Salut!

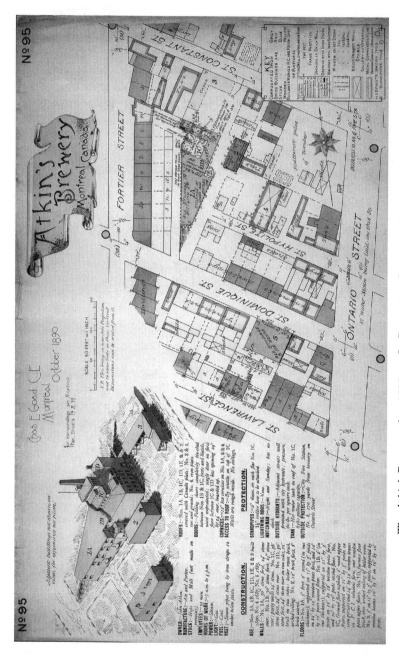

The Atkin's Brewery plan, 1890, on St. Dominique Street near Ontario. Fortier is probably Saint Norbert.

SALUT!

The Quebec Microbrewery Beer Cookbook

Raymond Beauchemin

Véhicule Press

Published with the assistance of the Book Publishing Industry Development Program of the Department of Canadian Heritage.

Cover design: JW Stewart
Cover photography: Thomas Leon Königsthal, Jr.
Photo of author: Sharon Musgrove
Special thanks: Frank Mrazik, Vicki Marcok, Rosemary Dardick
Set in Adobe Caslon by Simon Garamond
Printed by AGMV-Marquis Inc.

Images on pages 2, 151-52 are from the Rare Books and Special Collections Division, McGill University Libraries. All beer labels and other illustrations are from the collection of Frank Mrazik.

Recipe on pages 57-58 (© Lucy Saunders) is printed with the permission of Lucy Saunders. Quotation from *Charlevoix Country* (Penumbra Press) by Jori Smith used with permission.

Cataloguing in Publication Data

Beauchemin, Raymond
    Salut! : the Quebec microbrewery cookbook / Raymond Beauchemin.
ISBN 1-55065-155-2

1. Beer industry–Quebec (Province)–History. 2. Brewing industry–Quebec (Province)–History. 3. Microbreweries–Quebec (Province)–History. 4. Cookery (Beer) I. Title.

TP573.C3B42 2001   338.4'766342'09714   C2001-901045-1

Véhicule Press
www.vehiculepress.com

Canadian Distribution: LitDistCo, 100 Armstrong Avenue, Georgetown, Ontario, L7G 5S4 / 800-591-6250 / orders@litdistco.ca

U.S. Distribution: Independent Publishers Group, 814 North Franklin Street, Chicago, Illinois 60610 / 800-888-4741 / frontdesk@ipgbook.com / www.ipgbook.com

Printed in Canada

Contents

Invocation and Dedication 7

Preface 9

On Chemistry, Nutrition, Moulds and Other Sundries 11

Top Notes

        Styles of Beer in Quebec 15

        Substitution Chart 18

        Serving Beer, Pairing Beer 21

        Menu planner 24

Recipes

        Starters 27

        Soups 41

        Salads and Sides 53

        Main Dishes 63

            Pasta 64

            Poultry and Eggs 70

            Savoury Meats 83

            Stews and Chilis 90

            Fish and Seafood 97

        From the Bread Oven and Griddle 107

        Desserts 119

        Cheese and Beer: How Natural 131

        Drinks 137

A History, Comprehensive and Containing Certain Facts and

        Subjectivities, of Beer and Brewing in the Province of Quebec,

        From the Landing of Cartier to the Advent of Microbreweries 141

Passion 173

The Lees

        Websites 180

        Bibliography 182

Acknowledgements 186

Index 187

Invocation and Dedication

St. Arnold, or Arnulf as he is sometimes known, is generally accepted as the patron saint of brewers. But which St. Arnold? It is a historical fact that an Arnold was born to a prominent Austrian family in 580 and became bishop of Metz, France. According to legend, the good bishop spent his religious life warning peasants about the dangers of drinking water. Beer was safer, the churchman opined: "From man's sweat and God's love, beer came into the world." He died in 640. "A year later, the people of Metz requested that his body be exhumed and reburied in the Church of the Holy Apostles," wrote Brian Melton, the beer writer for the *Fort Worth Star-Telegram* in Texas. "During the arduous trip, the tired porters and followers stopped at a tavern in Champignuelles. There was only one mug of beer to be shared, but that mug never ran dry, and all the thirsty pilgrims were satisfied."

In his book, *Beer Companion*, Michael Jackson admits to the possibility of *two* Arnolds—neither of which is the bishop of Metz. He cites eleventh-century Benedictine monk-brewer, Arnold of Oudenaarde, and Arnold, bishop of Soissons, who was said to have ended a plague by immersing his crosier into a brew kettle.

The Brewers Association of Canada, in an attempt to clarify, limits Saint Arnold to being patron saint of brewers in Belgium, but further obfuscates the issue by declaring that three saints are named patrons of brewers: Augustine of Hippo, one of the most influential of the church's philosophers; Nicholas of Myra, whom most people know as Santa Claus; and the physician/evangelist Luke.

We must not forget Saint Thomas à Becket, the martyred archbishop of Canterbury, who took with him as gifts several barrels of English ale to persuade a French princess to accept Prince Henry as her husband in 1158. The act was enough to have a London guild, the Brewers' Company, name him their patron. And in another miracle reminiscent of the loaves and fishes, Saint Columban, while on a missionary tour of Germany, destroyed a cask of beer being drunk during a pagan worship ceremony. When the townspeople begged forgiveness of Columban, the priest took what little was left in the cask and served it to them, never running out. Saint Bridget, meanwhile, took her cue from Jesus' miracle at Cana by changing water into beer to quench the thirst of lepers.

It is with these holy men and women, all patrons of brewing, looking over my shoulder that I set about my brewing and cooking. I offer my next batch of beer to them.

As to this book, I dedicate it to my patron and partner in life and in the kitchen, my wife, Denise Roig. I'll clean up. I promise.

Preface

Historians, archæologists, and beer aficionados like to trace their favourite drink to a farmer's wife in Mesopotamia 7,000 years ago—give or take a century or two—who found that her container of barley, grain she used to make their daily bread, had become soaked in a heavy rain. She spread out the grain to let it dry in the desert sun. When she baked her bread later that day, she discovered it was sweeter than usual. The grain had undergone the beginning stages of malting.

The story goes that the family couldn't finish the barley bread that night, so they stored the leftovers in a clay pot that was also damp from the rain. The next morning the family noticed that foam had started to rise from the pot. Curious, the woman raised the pot and let the foam and liquid come to her lips. There it was. The first alcoholic beverage. Sweet and fermented. Beer.

No one will ever accuse me of letting the facts stand in the way of a good story. I am a journalist, after all. But the truth is we don't know when and where and how the first beer was made. The original beers were probably the accidental, spontaneous malting and fermentation of rain-soaked bread grains. The final product wouldn't have tasted anything like beers today or even those John Molson would have known in the eighteenth century. Hops, for example, though introduced into the brewing process around the time of Julius Caesar, weren't widely used until the sixteenth century. Before then, and through most of the Middle Ages, spices and herbs were used as preservatives and flavourings.

We do know one thing for sure, beer was made by women—one more responsibility on the list of household duties. Beer has been linked with cooking from its birth, and it is that link of history and imagination that this book celebrates.

This book is part history text, part cookbook. Think of it as a continuing tale of people who have left us a tradition worth cherishing.

My introduction to artisanal beers was in Massachusetts, where I was born. I came to love Samuel Adams beers—the flagship Boston lager, the creamy stout—and began to seek out similar brews on my travels. Searching for my French-Canadian roots, I arrived in Montreal in 1990 near the beginning of the craft-brewing movement in Quebec. Naturally, I gravitated toward the McAuslan, Boréale, Brasal, and GMT products that were available then. I also began brewing at home.

Eventually and inevitably, like a story without end, my beer-making turned into cooking. It was a natural path for my curiosity and taste buds to follow.

One autumn visit, my in-laws, Raphael and Jacky Roig, were our guests for a night of beer cuisine. The menu included, as it does almost every time my wife and I cook with beer, a delightful Weiss Dijon salad dressing from Lucy Saunders' vital collection of recipes, *Cooking With Beer*. Dessert, a chocolate torte, didn't seem to work, so Denise and I spent the next two years looking for the perfect beer dessert. The results are included in this book.

The night was special and I have wondered what made it that way. Was it the food, the beer, the company? Yes, but also the time we spend at the table, sitting and enjoying each course, each beer, and each other. Every dish has its own space and its own time, and its own beer as accompaniment. Time slows down, we relax, the beer flows.

In writing this book, I have tried to bring together my loves and interests: good beer, good food, and a good story. I am by no means an expert beer-taster or judge. I am neither a trained chef nor PhD-carrying historian. I am a journeyman beer drinker, homebrewer and home cook. I like what I like and am more than prepared to share these pleasures.

When I felt I did not know something about beer or cookery, I sought out experts, sometimes in person, sometimes in print. One subject of which I knew almost nothing, but which intrigued me, was the place of brewing in Quebec's history. I discovered a wealth of information in a variety of books, both in French and English. Nowhere was there a concise or complete history of beer and brewing in Quebec. Other facts were found in the pages of Canadian and Quebec literature. The story had to be told, so I have written a brief history tracing beer in Quebec from Jacques Cartier's scouting trips in the late 1500s to the craft-brewing phenomenon of the late 1990s.

A recipe is like a story. The ingredients are the characters; the methodology or cooking steps are the storyline that brings the characters together and drives them toward the inevitable denouement. And each recipe has a story inextricably connected to it, kind of like the off-camera experience of a character in a film or the history a novelist will give a character before setting him or her on the page.

As much as this book is about Quebec beer, food, and history, it is also about imagination. For that we should raise a glass. Salut!

Montreal, October 2003

On Chemistry, Nutrition, Moulds and Sundries

What strikes Anne Gardiner first about cooking with beer is the flavour. "I've tried beer breads with dramatically different beers just to see the difference in the flavour," she says. To prove her point, she tells the story of a friend who suggested a beer-bread recipe (who doesn't have one of those?) for a book she was co-writing, *The Inquisitive Cook*. Anne tried it out. It didn't work. Her writing partner tried it out. It didn't work. The beer just had off-flavours, the two felt. The reason? Trying to force a beer onto a recipe in which it did not complement the flavours of the other ingredients.

Anne has been writing about the chemistry of cooking for years with collaborator Sue Wilson. Their column, "The Inquisitive Cook," used to run in *The Gazette* in Montreal. The column spawned *The Inquisitive Cook*, a book published in 1998 by Henry Holt (distributed in Canada by Fitzhenry and Whiteside). Anne and Sue are now contributing editors at *Chatelaine* Magazine.

For Anne, one of the interesting chemical factors of beer is its Ph level. "Beer has a Ph of around four and five. Neutral is seven. Sour milk is four-and-a-half. So beer is fairly acidic. That has ramifications. Quick bread, for example, is made with baking soda or baking powder. Using beer, the acidity would complete the reaction with baking soda. Not with powder, however, because it already contains an acid," she says.

The acidity also enhances the action of the yeast. That's why in some bread recipes that require yeast, we find lemon juice among the ingredients. Beer, because of its acidity, can be used in place of the lemon juice.

Beer's acidity is also worth considering when cooking with cheese or simply pairing beer with a cheese. "That acidity is going to encourage the cheese to melt and blend. I'm thinking of a fondue," Anne says, "which always needs to have an acidic-enough wine, or lemon juice. Beer has that acidity."

When choosing a beer to accompany a cheese, consider the advice of beer writer Stephen Beaumont (*A Taste for Beer*): "Strong with strong and mild with mild." With this model in mind, have GMT's Belle Gueule with a bagel and cream cheese; Stilton or Danish blue cheese with Boréale Noire; Eau Bénite with Brick cheese; Raftman with Gruyère. There are as many cheeses available in Quebec as there are beers, so finding exactly the right match is a matter of trial-and-error. We'll get to cheese and beer later.

A third point to consider regarding chemistry is the body that beer brings to a dish. "In a soup," Anne says, "there's a real body there that you don't get with wine. Take a mouthful of beer. Roll your tongue through it, there's some substance there. Wine is more watery."

Beer with body is likely beer with some "muscle." "Using beer to braise a less-tender cut of beef helps tenderize that meat," Anne says. "You're getting into things like moist heat, breaking down the collagen that makes meat tough."

Now what about the alcohol content? Contrary to popular opinion, some alcohol does remain in a dish, depending on how long it is cooked, Anne says. "Because the boiling point is lowered, some people think all the alcohol is gone when they're just simmering the beer, but 40 percent to 80 percent can remain, depending on the length of cooking time."

This is not a cause for worry, however. What remains of the alcohol, if anything, adds to the overall taste—and that's the whole point.

One point that needs to be made regarding alcohol is calories. Much is made of beer's caloric heft—the image of the spare tire on the Canadian beer-guzzling man is stereotypical of the argument made against beer for this reason. The truth is, however, that there are fewer calories in a twelve-ounce bottle of lager, a Tremblay for instance, than a similar-sized glass of orange juice made from concentrate, apple juice, or two-percent milk. And stout, often having a lower alcohol level than lager, is even less calorific.

Top Notes

Frontenac Extra Stout, circa 1930. Stout, a dark beverage brewed with roasted malt is regaining popularity.

Styles of Beer in Quebec

There are many types and styles of beer. In Quebec, we are fortunate to have prolific, imaginative brewers that produce a wide range of these styles, as wide a range as can be found in New York/New England or California, whose populations (and numbers of brewers) are significantly larger.

The beers used in this cookbook are divided here by styles with general notes on the characteristics of that style plus ancillary notes on variations. Regardless of type, Le Cheval Blanc's ales are bottle-conditioned, or re-fermented, meaning that an active yeast remains in the bottle. And except for its Pilsners U and U2, the same goes for Unibroue. The yeast continues to age, adding complexity and a yeasty flavour to the unpasteurized, naturally carbonated beer.

Lager
Crisp beers with low taste profiles and little hop bitterness. However, Pilsner, a type of lager, is characterized by a distinct hop presence.

Belle Gueule, Tremblay (lagers)
Belle Gueule Rousse (red lager)
U (Pilsner)
U2 (red Pilsner)
Bière de Noël (strong spiced lager)

Canadian-style golden ale
Light to medium body, full flavour, golden colour that varies from straw to light amber.

Griffon, Illégal, Boréale Blonde, La Bolduc

Pale ale
Not pale at all, but copper in colour, with distinctive bitterness.

St. Ambroise Pale Ale

Amber and red ales
Darker and sweeter (maltier) and less bitter than pale ales.
Cheval Blanc Traditional Amber, Royale de L'Anse

Cheval Blanc Legendary Red, Boréale Rousse
Coup de Grisou (buckwheat, which is not a wheat at all, nor a cereal grass, but a plant whose seeds are made into cereal or flour, or in this case, malt!)

Scotch ale
Strong, almost syrupy, amber ales.

Loch Ness, McAuslan's Scotch Ale
Raftman (made with whisky malt) comes off smoky on the nose.

Brown ale
Nutty or caramel notes accompany this dark, reddish beer.

Griffon Brown

Stout
Roasted grains impart the darkness in this porter, which is lower in alcohol than many lighter-coloured beers and much less carbonated. There are four main stout styles: dry (or Irish) typified by Guinness; imperial (or Russian); sweet (also called milk) and oatmeal, which is relatively sweet.

St. Ambroise Oatmeal Stout
Boréale Noire (dry stout)

Strong ale
High in alcohol, generally dark and sweet.

Maudite, Trois Pistoles
Titanic, Blonde d'Achouffe, Boréale Cuivrée
McAuslan Vintage Ale, Unibroue's 11, Fringante, Terrible

Wheat beer
Wheat grain and unique yeasts give these bottle-refermented beers their special spiciness. The refermentation give these their hazy look. Wheat is the base malt for many beers and styles.

Blanche de Chambly, Tourmente (Belgian-style white, or wit)
1837 (strong Belgian-style white)
Don de Dieu (spiced winter wheat)
Cheval Blanc Original White (malty Belgian-style wit)
Rescousse (red wheat)

Tripel or triple
Three fermentations (the last in the bottle), with a light-to-medium colour, neutral hop/malt balance, mousseline head and perceived alcohol taste.

La Fin du Monde

Abbey ale
A strong beer on yeast brewed in a traditional Belgian monastery style. High in alcohol; blond, amber or brown in colour.

Eau Bénite (the draught version is lower in alcohol than the bottle-refermented one that gets three fermentations, qualifying this as a tripel as well).

Flavoured or fruit ales
A whole range of subtle fruit flavours. In Quebec, we're lucky that none of the fruit or flavoured ales from the major brewers tastes like soda. Sometimes these beers are made with the actual fruit itself, or with fruit syrup. In the case of the maple and honey beers, they are made with the syrups.

Tord-vis (maple—available in spring)
Sainte-Paix (cherry wheat—available in summer)
Sainte-Paix (apple—available in fall)
Quelque Chose (cherry lambic)
Apricot wheat (apricot)
Boréale Douce (honey)
Folie Douce (blueberry)
Snoreau (cranberry)
Ephémère (apple, peach, original)

A note on availability
In Quebec, the following are available only in SAQ (liquor board) outlets: Tourmente, Titanic, Rescousse, McAuslan's Scotch Ale, Quelque Chose.

Substitution Chart

Not all beers are available everywhere. Sad. But true. Especially in Canada! If you live in a Canadian province other than Quebec, or if you live in the United States where some Quebec beers are not distributed, it might be difficult getting your hands on the beers used as ingredients in this book. This easy-to-follow chart, categorized by type or style of beer, can help you find a suitable beer. I've tried to substitute beers that would be more readily available. There's no point in subbing one esoteric beer for another, right? This list is drawn from beers made in Canada and the United States, plus some popular imports. No doubt, you have favourites of your own that will do just fine. When in doubt, use the old rule about wine: the lighter the meat, the lighter the wine or beer.

If the recipe calls for	*Use*
Lager	
Belle Gueule or Tremblay	Creemore Springs Premium Lager, Pete's Gold Coast, Stella Artois, Grolsch Premium, Brick Premium Lager, Great Western Premium Lager
U (Pilsner)	Moretti, Samuel Adams Golden Pilsner, Labatt Blue, Köld, Heineken, Upper Canada Lager, Corona
U (red Pilsner)	Dos Equis, Upper Canada Rebellion
Belle Gueule Rousse (red lager)	Samuel Adams Boston Lager, Algonquin County Lager, Upper Canada Rebellion Lager, Climax ESB

Winter Lager
Bière de Noël (strong lager)   Samuel Adams Winter Lager

Smoked or spiced ale
Raftman (made with whisky malt)   Any smoked or rachbier

Canadian-style golden ale
Illégal, La Bolduc   Molson Export, Labatt 50, John Labatt Classic, Atlantic Storm IPA, Halifax 1749 Stoned Fired Ale, Moosehead

Pale Ale
St. Ambroise   Pete's Wicked Ale, Pyramid Pale Ale, Red Hook (ESB), Sierra Nevada Pale Ale, Bass, Alaskan ESB, Samuel Adams Boston Ale, Granville Island IPA, Hart Festive Brown, Arkel Best Bitter

Griffon, Boréale Blonde   Saranac Pale Ale, Samuel Smith Pale Ale, Alexander Keith's IPA, Big Rock Warthog Ale, Upper Canada Dark

Amber
Cheval Blanc Traditional Amber or Royale de L'Anse   Saranac-Adirondack Amber Ale, Rickard's Red, Gastown Amber Ale, Hart Amber

Red
Cheval Blanc Legendary Red   Eldgridge Pope Royal Oak, Conners Best Bitter, Big Rock Traditional Ale, Shaftbury Rainforest Amber

Brown ale
Griffon Brown   Otter Creek Wolaver's Brown, Samuel Smith Nut Brown, Newcastle Brown, Waterloo Dark Lager, Muskoka Premium Dark, Sleeman's Original Dark

Scotch Ale

Loch Ness or McAuslan's

McRogue Scotch, Samuel Adams Scottish, Long Trail Hibernator Ale, McEwan's

Stout

St. Ambroise Oatmeal

Samuel Smith Celebrated Oatmeal, Young's Oatmeal

Boréale Noire

Rogue Shakespeare Stout, Brock's Extra Stout, Guinness, Sierra Nevada Stout, Bell's Porter

Strong Ale

Maudite

Trois Pistoles

Titanic or Boréale Cuivrée

Don de Dieu, McAuslan's Vintage Ale

Duvel, Celis Grand Cru

Dogfish Head Raison d'Etre

Theakston Old Peculiar, Fuller's Golden Pride, McNally's Extra Ale Harpoon Winter Warmer

Wheat Beer

Blanche de Chambly (Belgian-style white), 1837 (strong), Tourmente or Cheval Blanc Original White

Celis White, Blanche des Bruges, Allagash White

Triple

La Fin du Monde or Blonde McChouffe

Celis Grand Cru, New Belgium Trippel, Allagash Triple Reserve, Dogfish Head Midas Touch

Abbey ale

Eau Bénite

Saint Sixtus

Flavoured ales

Tord-Vis (maple)

Sainte-Paix (cherry wheat)

Apricot wheat (apricot)

Snoreau (cranberry)

La Beauceronne à l'Erable

Samuel Adams Cherry Wheat

Pyramid Apricot Ale

Samuel Adams Cranberry Lambic

Serving Beer, Pairing Beer

This is where the enjoyment of artisanal beers verges on snobbishness. I remember when having a beer with friends meant reaching into a refrigerator for an ice-cold can of Bud, popping it open (there's almost nothing quite as distinctive sounding as that thin metal ring and the explosion of carbonation escaping into the air), then plopping down on a buddy's couch in front of the television. We're still allowed to do that, of course, but when everyone else is at the dinner table, it's kind of rude to be watching hockey.

So now we've got rules about the right temperature for storing and serving beer, the right type of glass, the correct angle at which to tip said glass and where to aim the beer: whether down the side of the glass or in the centre.

Why all the fuss about glassware? First, because you want to see the beer, its clarity and colour and the head of foam; secondly, only the right-shaped glass will capture and concentrate all of a beer's flavours.

The right type of glassware adds to the experience, Stephen Beaumont told me once in a St. Laurent Boulevard brewpub. "You can have a vintage Bordeaux in a jam jar and it will taste the same as if you had it in nice stemware. But, to fully appreciate the aroma and colour of beer, you need the right glass. Otherwise you're denying yourself part of the experience."

Pouring an aromatic beer in a fluted glass, for example, might deny you the pleasure of the nose because its head will be too thick for the aroma to rise to you. A Trappist ale, another example, should be drunk in a Trappist ale glass, which is shaped, not surprisingly, like a chalice. An ice-cold mug from the freezer might be ideal to keep a beer cold in the summer, but all it really does is dilute the beer with water as the ice melts and freeze your tastebuds. Avoid them at a beer tasting. Of course, these are just guidelines. If you don't have the right glass, the Unibroue police aren't about to bust you. Those pewter tankards are just fine.

But if you're committed to doing it properly, here are a few hints:

For **Belgian ale**, use a tulip-shaped glass or a chalice-shaped goblet.
For **stout**, use a simple pint glass as you'd find in a British or Irish pub.
For **strong ale**, like barleywine, old ale or imperial stout, use a brandy snifter.

For **fruit beer**, use thin, stemmed flutes.
For **Pilsner** and **wit**, use a tall, narrow glass.
For **wheat beer**, a thick-walled, tall glass.
For **Scotch ale**, a thistle-shaped glass.

In general, when trying out tastings of your own, you will want to start out the evening with lighter beers and move toward the darker, heavier ones. Also in general—because there are exceptions to every rule—you'll be pairing lighter beers with lighter dishes. For example, game meats like venison go well with a strong ale like Trois Pistoles, which enhances the meat's richness but undercuts its gaminess. For some fruit beers, you might consider what the fruit would naturally have gone with. Snoreau cranberry ale, for example, works with turkey; Sainte-Paix cherry beer with rabbit or ham.

Scotch ales and stouts are generally the beer of choice for dessert, having the requisite end-of-meal sweetness. Perhaps the best after-meal drink, however, on par with a brandy or Armagnac, would be Quelque Chose, warmed in a double-boiler to about 70 degrees F (158° C) and drunk from espresso cups. McAuslan brewed a high-in-alcohol vintage "Millennial" beer for the year 2000. The bottles are collector's items, numbered individually, signed by brewer Ellen Bounsall and boxed. They're great for after dinner, or before, and like several of the Unibroue beers, can be stored for up to ten years or so.

Here are other pairing hints:

Lagers, Pilsners and light-bodies ales
Appetizers and hors d'œuvres, fish, sushi, sausage, pizza

Pale ale
Roast chicken, shellfish, fish, hamburgers, barbecues, roast beef, lamb, Thai or Indian spicy food, sushi, salad

Amber and red ales
Shrimp, chicken, beef stew, vegetable soups, barbecue

Wheat beer
Salads, raw vegetables, pasta, poultry and fowl, rabbit, pork, fish and crustaceans, fruits, sorbets, terrines

Scotch ale
Smoked fish and meats, chili, mildly spicy dishes, dessert

Brown ale
Roast beef, veal, lamb, pork, hamburgers, game

Belgian (Trappist, abbey ale)
Game

Belgian fruit ale
Fruit pie or tart, sweet dessert

Strong ale
Pasta, red meat, spicy dishes, game, post-dinner cigar

Stout or porter
Chocolate, desserts, cheesecake, caviar, crustaceans, oysters, salmon, barbecue

Menu Planner

Honey, what time are the Troy-Adamses coming over? AHHHHH! Nothing worse than not being prepared, except perhaps the haggling over what dishes to make for a beer-tasting and cooking night. Relax. Whatever decision you make—from a choice of beer "mate" to what to put on the menu—is the right decision.

The idea behind a degustatory evening is to take advantage of as many of Quebec's beer styles as possible in one sitting. You're not going to be able to do them all in one evening, so let your taste buds and instincts be your guide.

These are some menu suggestions taken from this book. You'll want to try others using the pairing guide that precedes this, and the substitution chart if needed.

Above all, the key is moderation. Limit your accompanying beers to about four ounces, about 125 mL (three people to one bottle).

Boréale Black Bean Gazpacho
(accompanied by Boréale Rousse)
Warm Salad of Smoked Duck,
Quelque Chose Couscous and Napa Cabbage
(accompanied by Quelque Chose)
Chocolate Stout Mousse
(accompanied by St. Ambroise Oatmeal Stout)

Mussels de Richelieu alongside Belgian-style Fries With Mayonnaise
(accompanied by Blanche de Chambly)
Apricot Chicken Pilaf With Almonds
(accompanied by McAuslan Apricot wheat beer)
Strawberry Cherry Soup
(accompanied by Sainte-Paix)
Cheese Plate
(follow serving suggestion Cheese & Beer section)

Chinese Shrimp Rolls
(accompanied by Belle Gueule)
Trout Roulade With Asparagus
(accompanied by McAuslan Scotch Ale)
McAuslan's Mixed Greens and Danish Blue Cheese Salad
(accompanied by Boréale Noire)
Cheddar and Ale Cheesecake (accompanied by La Fin du Monde)

Hummus bi-Tahini bi-Cheval Blanc and Tabouleh
(accompanied by Tremblay)
Scallops With Couscous
(accompanied by La Maudite)
Salad with Blueberry Vinaigrette
(accompanied by Folie Douce)
Cherry Zabaglione
(followed by Quelque Chose, warmed)

Carling's beers can still be found, though they are now brewed by Molson.

Recipes

Starters

Mussels de Richelieu

This dish was originally called Mussels Brugeoises after the Blanche de Bruges Belgian beer that was used to make it. It is a variation on a creation of Chef Éric Lehousse of Le Petit Moulinsart, a restaurant in Old Montreal that features, in its décor and menu, the cartoon character Tintin. If using a Quebec beer, Chef Lehousse suggests using Unibroue's Blanche de Chambly, named after the town and fort on the Richelieu River.

2 pounds (1 kg) mussels
½ stalk celery, coarsely chopped
½ leek, coarsely chopped
2 slices onion, coarsely chopped
3 slices orange, including rind, each slice quartered
1 bottle (12 oz./341 mL) Blanche de Chambly
Pinch of salt
Pinch of pepper

1. Scrub and beard mussels. Discard any that are already open. Place celery, leek, onion and orange in a 2-quart (2L) pot. Add mussels. Pour in beer, but do not cover mussels. Salt and pepper to taste.

2. Boil, covered, until mussels begin to open. Toss lightly so that mussels on top can have turn at the bottom. Boil for a minute longer.

3. Serve as soon as all mussels have opened, discarding any that haven't.

Mussels au Gratin with Stout

SERVES 2 TO 3

What connaisseur and writer Michael Jackson is to the world of beer, Mario d'Eer is to beer in Quebec. Nonpareil. His recipe for Mussels au Gratin with Stout is without equal as well. The original recipe called for a can of Guinness, but he suggests using Boréale Noire if using a Quebec beer, and St. Ambroise Oatmeal Stout as accompaniment.

1 bottle (12 oz./341 mL) Boréale Noire
2 stalks celery, diced
1 leek, white part only, sliced thinly
1 large carrot, peeled and diced
1 small onion, diced
Freshly ground pepper to taste
2 pounds (1 kg) mussels, washed and cleaned
1 tablespoon (15 mL) cornmeal
1 cup (250 mL) 15% cream
7 tablespoons (105 mL) Emmenthal cheese, grated

1. In a large pot bring the beer, vegetables, and pepper to a boil. Lower the heat and simmer 5 minutes.

2. Add the mussels and cook until they open, discarding any that do not. Drain and reserve 2 tablespoons (30 mL) of the cooking liquid in a small pot. Remove mussels from their shells. Set aside shells for use later.

3. Warm the reserved liquid. Mix together the cornmeal and cream, then add to the warming liquid. Whisk until thickened, 5 to 8 minutes.

4. Preheat the oven to 400° F (200° C). Arrange the shells on a baking sheet. Place one mussel on each half-shell. Add sauce with some of the boiled vegetables. Top with grated cheese. Bake until cheese melts. Serve immediately.

Kick-Ass Mussels
(Moules Qui Galopent)

SERVES 2 TO 3

Wine is used in the classic preparation of mussels. This recipe is one reason not to. These mussels, made with Le Cheval Blanc's Titanic, can serve as an appetizer for several people, or as a meal for two. Best served with fries and mayonnaise, for a traditional Belgian meal.

1 bottle (12 oz./341 mL) Titanic
½ onion, coarsely chopped
1 clove garlic, chopped
2 pounds (1 kg) mussels, washed and cleaned
1 cup (250 mL) plain yogurt
¼ teaspoon (1 mL) curry powder
1 tablespoon (15 mL) fresh dill, chopped
¼ teaspoon (1 mL) salt
½ teaspoon (2 mL) celery pepper

1. Bring the beer to a boil in a 4-quart pot. Add onion and garlic, then simmer for one minute. Add the mussels, stir and cover. Cook for three minutes, stirring once every minute.

2. When the mussels have opened, remove from heat. Discard any unopened mussels. With a slotted spoon, remove mussels to a large bowl. Reserve one-half cup (125 mL) of the cooking liquid. Refrigerate the liquid one hour.

3. In a bowl, mix the yogurt, curry, dill, salt and celery pepper. Add the cooled liquid.

4. Shell the mussels and reserve a third of the shells. Fold the mussels into the yogurt mixture and let rest at room temperature for 30 minutes.

5. Place three mussels in each shell. Pour remaining yogurt mixture over mussels. Serve immediately, refrigerate until mealtime, or heat in the oven (350° F) for seven minutes and serve immediately.

Shrimp and Onion Rings
in Belle Gueule Batter

SERVES 2 TO 4

A beer batter is one of the traditional ways of cooking with beer. What is nice about this batter is how truly light it is—and that's partly the presence of the Belle Gueule, a lager from Brasseurs GMT. The paprika provides some added colour.

3 large Spanish onions
1 pound (500 grams) large shrimp
3 large eggs
2 cups (500 mL) Belle Gueule
3 cups (750 mL) all-purpose flour
1 tablespoon (15 mL) salt
1 teaspoon (5 mL) white pepper
1 teaspoon (5 mL) paprika
Oil for deep frying

1. Peel onions. Cut in half-inch slices and pop out rings. Use only the larger rings for this recipe.

2. Peel and de-vein the shrimp.

3. Beat the eggs and add beer slowly, beating lightly all the while. Sift flour and seasonings then whisk into egg mixture.

4. Heat the oil in deep frying pan until it is hot, but not smoking, about 375° F.

5. Dip the shrimp, one by one, into the batter, shake off the excess then fry in hot oil until golden brown. Follow the same procedure with the onion rings. Wait until the oil has reached 375° F before adding more shrimp or rings. Drain on a paper towel.

Escabèche

Today, we are prone to the egocentric notion that the Wright brothers invented travel. A glance at historical migration proves otherwise. And so does the escabèche (*scavece* in Italy; *escavèche* in Belgium), which spread throughout the Mediterranean, North Africa, and Chile. No longer solely a fish dish, variations can include chicken and game birds like partridge.

2 cups (500 mL) Eau Bénite
½ cup (125 mL) white wine vinegar
Salt to taste
1 pound (500 g) turbot or other white fish
1 Spanish onion, diced
1 large carrot, diced
3 threads of saffron
¼ teaspoon (1 mL) ground cumin
¼ teaspoon (1 mL) ground pepper
¼ teaspoon (1 mL) paprika

1. Boil the beer with the vinegar and salt. Add fish, lower the heat and simmer covered, for 10 minutes. Remove the fish to a shallow dish.

2. Add the onion and carrot to the liquid, return to a boil, then lower heat until liquid reduces by two-thirds. Remove from heat and add the saffron, cumin, pepper, paprika and more salt if desired. Pour over the fish, and marinate a minimum of six hours. (Traditionally, it was marinated for 24 hours.) Just before serving remove from marinade and serve cold.

Belgian Fries with Mayonnaise

Move over ketchup, you *too* vinegar! Belgians, the French, and an increasing number of Quebecers prefer to dip their fries in mayonnaise (preferably home-made). Dijon, tarragon, sun-dried tomatoes, capers, paprika, garlic, pesto, Tex-Mex, and curry are just some of the flavoured mayos popular in Montreal restaurants.

Mayonnaise
2 egg yolks
1 egg
1 tablespoon (15 mL) Dijon mustard
Pinch salt
Ground black pepper to taste
2 tablespoons (30 mL) 1837
¼ cup (60 mL) lemon juice
2 cups (500 mL) olive oil

Combine the yolks, egg, mustard, salt, pepper, beer, and lemon juice in a food processor and blend for one minute. Add the oil in a thin stream while mixing. Shut off processor and scrape sides of bowl. Taste and adjust seasoning or lemon juice. Blend a few seconds more if needed. Remove to another bowl and refrigerate. Will keep up to five days.

Fries
2 large, washed and scrubbed golden potatoes per person
Oil for deep-frying

1. Heat oil in a fryer or wok to 375° F.

2. Slice potatoes lengthwise, then halve (again lengthwise) the larger slices. Place in hot oil and fry until golden brown. Remove to paper towels. Return oil to 375° F before adding new slices.

3. Serve immediately with mayonnaise.

Hummus bi-Tahini bi-Cheval Blanc

SERVES 3 TO 4

The phrase "breaking bread" is synonymous with a bond forming between people, strangers coming together and becoming friends; friends and family whose relationships deepen with every meal shared; with "communion" in its religious and secular meanings. The same feeling resonates with a communal bowl of hummus: broken pieces of pita dipped in, scooping up dollops of the thick, garlicky garbanzo-bean paste. Simply prepared, simply presented, simply delicious.

2 large cloves garlic
½ teaspoon (2 mL) salt
½ cup (125 mL) lemon juice
3 rounded tablespoons (50 mL) tahini
1 can (19 ounces/540 mL) chickpeas, drained and rinsed
¼ cup (60 mL) Cheval Blanc Original White Beer
½ teaspoon (2 mL) olive oil
Paprika
Pita

1. Blend garlic and salt in a blender or food processor for 10 seconds.

2. Add lemon juice and tahini and process for another 10 seconds.

3. Reserve a dozen chickpeas.

4. Add chickpeas and beer and blend until smooth.

5. Pour mixture into a bowl and flatten with a spatula or back of a spoon. Drizzle olive oil in a circle on top and sprinkle with a dash or two of paprika. Decorate with reserved chickpeas.

6. Preheat the oven to 350° F. Tear pita breads into bite-sized dipping pieces and place on a baking sheet. Bake until crisp, and then serve with hummus.

Poppers and Fritters

SERVES 4 TO 6

Have plenty of friends over and ice-cold beer ready before you eat these jalapeño poppers.

1⅓ cups (330 mL) all-purpose flour, sifted
1 teaspoon (5 mL) sugar
1 teaspoon (5 mL) salt
¼ teaspoon (1 mL) white pepper
1 tablespoon (15 mL) vegetable oil
2 eggs, separated
¾ cup (180 mL) La Bolduc
24 jalapeño peppers, stemmed and seeded
Cream cheese

1. Combine the dry ingredients, then add the oil and well-beaten egg yolks. Mix thoroughly. Add the beer slowly, constantly stirring.

2. In a separate bowl, beat the egg whites until stiff. Fold into the batter mixture.

3. Stuff each pepper with cream cheese (flavoured if you want). Dip each pepper into the batter and coat well.

4. At this point, you can bake these in the oven at 350° F degrees until the peppers are golden brown, or deep-fry them in hot oil until golden.

A Variation—Apple Fritters

This same batter can be used to coat just about anything. A favourite of mine are apple fritters. Peel, core, and slice four medium apples. Dip in batter, coat, deep fry until golden, then sprinkle generously with powdered sugar.

Nessie's Riblets

There are two things I like about this recipe. One is the size of the ribs, which was an accident. I had asked my butcher to give me three racks of pork ribs, separated. They came back separated, but cut into bite-size pieces. Then there is the sauce itself, which is tangy and sweet. The sauce, good anywhere you would normally use barbecue sauce, will keep a couple of weeks.

These riblets, made with Loch Ness Scottish ale from Le Cheval Blanc, are served with Red Line Chili (see page 92), and are accompanied by Illégal, a light lager from Brasseurs de l'Anse.

1 medium onion, finely chopped

2 cloves garlic, minced

2 tablespoons bacon drippings

1 bottle (14 ounce/350 mL) regular ketchup

2 tablespoons (30 mL) red wine vinegar

⅔ cup (160 mL) Loch Ness

1 tablespoon (15 mL) Worcestershire sauce

¼ cup (60 mL) molasses (or dark malt extract)

Salt and coarsely ground black pepper, to taste

2 tablespoons (30 mL) Dijon mustard

1 cup (250 mL) barbecue sauce (your favourite will do)

Tabasco to taste

½ teaspoon (2 mL) liquid smoke

3 racks of pork ribs, separated and cut into bite-size pieces

1. Sauté the onion and garlic in the bacon drippings until translucent.

2. In a one-quart (litre) pot add the remaining ingredients except the liquid smoke and ribs. Bring to a boil, add the liquid smoke, then simmer gently for 15 minutes. Remove from heat and refrigerate until ready to use.

3. Boil ribs in water for 40 minutes, then drain. Preheat oven to 375° F degrees. Place rib pieces in a baking pan. Cover with barbecue sauce and bake for 45 minutes, turning once.

Chinese Shrimp Rolls

Spring rolls were traditionally prepared for Spring Festivals in China and Vietnam. But North America has adopted spring rolls as a mandatory Chinese takeout appetizer any time of the year. This is an adaptation of a recipe prepared for the Brewers Association of Canada dinner in December 1999.

⅔ pound (300 g) Matane or Nordic shrimp, cleaned and chopped
¾ pound (375 g) scallops, diced
1 bottle (12 oz./341 mL) Griffon Blonde
1 large onion, finely chopped
1 large red pepper, finely chopped
2 tablespoons (30 mL) chives or parsley, finely chopped
2 cloves garlic, minced
Salt and pepper to taste
Spring roll wrappers
Oil for deep frying

1. Poach the pieces of shrimp and scallop in the beer and seasonings until scallops are cooked through. Remove with a slotted spoon.

2. Simmer the chopped onion, pepper, parsley and garlic in the beer until the liquid is reduced by three-quarters.

3. Mix the cooked vegetables and seafood together in a bowl. Lay out spring roll wrapper so that it faces you in the shape of a diamond. Place about 1½ tablespoons (23 mL) of the mixture in the centre of the wrapper. Fold the bottom point of the diamond over the mixture, about two-thirds of the way to the top. Hold this in place while tucking in the left and right corners together to seal ends. Now roll the pastry toward the top. Repeat this until you've run out of mixture.

4. Heat oil in a deep-fryer, deep skillet, or a wok. Place five or six spring rolls into the oil and cook until golden brown. Remove with tongs or a slotted spoon onto a baking sheet covered with paper towels. Repeat until all are cooked. Serve with soy sauce flavoured with garlic, lemon juice, and chopped coriander.

Vegetable Plate with Boréale
Blue Cheese Dip

This smooth, creamy dip with a distinct blue-cheese sharpness makes a great appetizer paired with Boréale Blonde or even a sturdier beer, such as a pale ale.

1 pound (500 g) creamy blue cheese at room temperature
⅔ cup (160 mL) cream cheese at room temperature
⅓ cup (80 mL) 10% cream
3 tablespoons (45 mL) Boréale Blonde
¼ teaspoon (1 mL) white pepper
1 pinch celery salt
Ripe black olives, sliced

1. Combine the cheeses with a fork. Blend in the cream, beer, pepper, and salt. Mix until smooth. Spoon the dip into a bowl and refrigerate at least one hour.

2. Garnish with black olives.

Serve with assorted crackers, carrot and celery sticks, sweet peppers, cauliflower or broccoli, radishes, and other vegetables.

Mushrooms and Brie in Pastry

This recipe was created by Montreal Chef Rick Spensieri for a beer gastronomy night featuring McAuslan beers. Brie in phyllo pastry makes a wonderful appetizer. The addition of mushrooms sautéed with St. Ambroise Pale Ale is a natural complement.

¼ cup (60 mL) butter
2 cups (500 mL) sliced button mushrooms
1 clove garlic, minced
Salt and pepper to taste
1 bottle (12 oz./341 mL) St. Ambroise Pale Ale
6 sheets phyllo pastry
¼ cup (60 mL) melted butter
½ pound (250 g) sliced brie

1. Melt the butter in a sauce pan and sauté the mushrooms and garlic. Add salt and pepper. Add the beer and cook over medium heat until the beer is almost completely reduced.

2. Lay out a sheet of phyllo pastry and brush with melted butter. Lay a second sheet of phyllo over the first, brush with butter and cover with a third sheet. Cut the phyllo into individual squares, cutting in half by length first then in thirds across. Place a slice of brie in the centre of each pastry square with a spoonful of the mushroom mixture. Wrap into small bundles. Repeat, to create five more squares. Bake at 350° F degrees until golden and crisp.

An example of a Molson's playing card, 1925.

Soups

Baked Potato Soup

T here really isn't any better way to bake potatoes than in aluminum foil. The foil incubates at the same time as it preserves any moisture that might otherwise escape the potato.

8 medium baking potatoes
1 teaspoon (5 mL) olive oil
1 tablespoon (15 mL) butter
2 stalks celery, chopped
1 medium onion, chopped
1 tablespoon (15 mL) each, fresh parsley, dill, chopped
Salt and freshly ground black pepper to taste
1 bottle (12 oz./341 mL) Blanche de Chambly

For white sauce
2 cups (500 mL) whole milk
¼ cup (60 mL) butter
6 tablespoons (90 mL) flour
½ cup (125 mL) 10% cream

Parsley for garnish

1. Bake the potatoes in aluminum foil at 400 degrees for 40 to 45 minutes, until a fork enters potato without struggle. Remove from oven and cool on a rack.

2. While the potatoes are cooling, heat the oil and butter in a sauce pan. Sauté the celery and onion over medium-high heat until translucent.

3. While the celery and onion are cooking, dice potatoes into half-inch cubes. Add the potatoes, parsley, dill, salt and pepper and ¼ cup (60 mL) of the beer. Let heat over low heat.

4. In a separate sauce pan, heat the milk to boiling, being careful that it doesn't scorch or boil over.

5. While the milk is being brought to a boil, melt the tablespoon (15 mL) of butter in another sauce pan. Stir in the flour slowly, stirring for about five minutes. Add all of the boiled milk, raise heat to medium and bring the mixture to a low boil, stirring constantly, for about five minutes.

6. Add the thickened sauce to the potatoes, mix and add the cream and the rest of the bottle of beer. Heat through over low heat. Pour into bowls and garnish with fresh parsley.

Illégal Black Bean Gazpacho

SERVES 8

A variation on a theme of gazpacho, this time with Illégal and black beans giving this spicy soup its body.

1 can (19 oz./540 mL) tomato juice
1 cup (250 mL) Illégal
1 large red pepper, seeded and diced
1 chipotle (smoked jalapeño) pepper, diced
2 cloves garlic, minced
3 large tomatoes, chopped coarsely
4 scallions including green part, chopped,
¼ cup (60 mL) chopped fresh coriander
2 tablespoons (30 mL) olive oil
2 tablespoons (30 mL) red wine vinegar
Salt and pepper to taste
Jalapeño cream

1. Combineall ingredients except jalapeño cream and chill two to three hours before serving. Add a dollop of jalapeño cream to each bowl (recipe below).

Jalapeño Cream

This cream is designed for combining in creamy soups like Carrot and Sweet Potato Soup, Roasted Squash Soup, or Black Bean Gazpacho.

1 or 2 jalapeño peppers, depending on desired heat, seeded and chopped
1 scallion, chopped
1 cup (250 mL) sour cream or 10% yogurt
½ teaspoon (2 mL) salt
3 tablespoons (45 mL) 10% cream

Blend in a blender until smooth and chill before using.

Carrot and Sweet Potato Soup

SERVES 8

Almost nothing warms my heart and stomach the way a good soup does. This is my favourite. Enough said.

2 pounds (1 kg) carrots, peeled or scrubbed, sliced thinly
2 sweet potatoes, sliced thinly
3 cups (750 mL) water
1 bottle (12 oz./341 mL) bottle McAuslan Apricot wheat
1 heaping teaspoon (6 mL) salt
4 tablespoons (60 mL) butter
2 medium onions
2 large cloves garlic, minced
⅓ cup (80 mL) almonds
½ cup (125 mL) 35% cream
½ cup (125 mL) sour cream
1 tablespoon (15 mL) fresh tarragon
1 tablespoon (15 mL) fresh basil
1 tablespoon (15 mL) fresh thyme

1. Place the carrots and potatoes in a pot with the water and beer. Add salt and bring to a boil. Cover and allow to simmer over low heat 15 minutes.

2. Sauté onions, garlic and almonds until onions are translucent. Add to cooked carrots.

3. Purée all until smooth. Return to the pot while whisking in the cream. Heat through, but don't boil. Season with herbs. Taste and add salt and pepper if needed.

Eau Bénite Summer Cucumber Soup

There's the scene in the frathouse farce *Animal House* in which Tim Matheson's character, Otter, attempts to seduce the wife of the college dean, played by Verna Bloom, in the produce section of a grocery store. He turns to her, cucumber in hand, fleshy and firm, its green skin shiny and smooth, and asks, "Vegetables can be really sensuous, don't you think?" And Bloom, in one of the classic rejoinders of a come-on, says: "No. Vegetables are sensual. *People* are sensuous."

Summer soups pique the senses in a way almost no other soup can. In the heat and oppressive mugginess of summer, they cool and refresh. This soup, using fresh cucumber and dill and the slightly vegetal, triple-fermented Eau Bénite triple ale of Unibroue, dances lightly on the tongue, an homage to the season and the senses.

The lemon zest in this recipe can be substituted with curry if you're seeking an Indian flavour; or use yogurt instead of the sour cream and kick in some minced garlic with the onion for a soup with a hint of Greece.

1 tablespoon (15 mL) olive oil
1 cup (250 mL) onion, chopped
3 cups (750 mL) cucumber, peeled, seeded and diced
1 cup (250 mL) Eau Bénite
1 cup (250 mL) chicken stock
1 cup (250 mL) sour cream (or plain yogurt)
2 tablespoons (30 mL) chopped fresh dill
1 teaspoon (5 mL) lemon zest
Salt and freshly ground pepper to taste
Freshly chopped parsley or chives for garnish

1. Heat the oil in a saucepan over medium heat and sauté the onion until tender. Add the cucumber, beer and stock. Bring to a boil, then reduce heat to a simmer for five minutes. Cool to lukewarm. This is necessary so the sour cream won't curdle when you add it to the heated cucumber liquid.

2. Purée the cucumber and stock in a blender. Pour into a bowl, whisk in sour cream until smooth. Add dill, zest, salt and pepper. Chill until ready to serve with garnish.

French Onion Soup

What I love about French onion soup is also what I struggle with most. The cheese. How do you, with any kind of decorum, actually get those goopy globs or stretchy strings into your mouth? And since most people don't make French onion soup at home, this breach of etiquette usually happens in a restaurant. Serve this exceptionally smooth French onion soup at home, it solves the cheese problem and will more than impress your guests.

5 cups (1.25 L) chicken broth
1 bottle (12 oz./341 mL) Boréale Cuivrée or strong ale
1 tablespoon (15 mL) fresh thyme leaves
A few sprigs of parsley, chopped
Crushed bay leaf
5 tablespoons (75 mL) butter
3 cups (750 mL) onions, sliced thinly
4 scallions, greens included, sliced thinly,
Salt and freshly ground pepper to taste
3 tablespoons (45 mL) cognac (optional, but oh, what an option)
1 baguette of French bread, in half-inch slices
½ cup (125 mL) mild goat cheese, sliced

1. In a soup pot, heat the broth, beer and herbs. Set aside when hot but not boiling.

2. Melt butter in skillet. Add onions and scallions; salt and pepper. Cook over medium-low heat for 20 minutes. Add cognac and cook for another 10 minutes.

3. Add golden-brown onions to broth and continue cooking over medium-low heat for another 30 minutes.

4. Meanwhile, preheat oven to 375 degrees. Place bread slices on a cookie sheet or baking tray with one slice of cheese atop each slice of bread. Toast until golden.

5. Ladle soup into bowls. Add two or three toasted slices of bread and cheese to each bowl. Garnish with parsley if desired.

Damned Gazpacho

Maudite means "damned" in English and this is a damned-fine spicy beer, with a nice nose-hint of cloves. It's perfect inside and outside of gazpacho, a spicy Spanish soup.

3½ cups (875 mL) tomato juice (or V-8 for added spice)
½ cup (125 mL) Maudite
2 cups (500 mL) diced tomatoes
1 small onion, finely chopped
2 scallions, including green leaves, chopped
1 cucumber, peeled, seeded and diced
1 clove minced garlic
1 teaspoon (5 mL) light malt extract
2 tablespoons (25 mL) olive oil
2 tablespoons (25 mL) red wine vinegar
Juice of ½ lemon and 1 lime
Dash of ground cumin
Dash of red curry paste
Dash of liquid smoke
¼ cup (60 mL) fresh parsley or chervil, chopped
1 tablespoon each (15 mL) fresh cut tarragon and basil
Salt and pepper to taste

1. Combine all ingredients and chill a few hours before serving.

Stout Minestrone

The vegetarian version of this workhorse soup is so chockfull of flavour and ingredients, it has on occasion seemed stewlike to me. If you like your minestrone more souplike, though, add a bit more vegetable stock.

3 tablespoons (45 mL) olive oil
1 cup (250 mL) onion, chopped
5 cloves garlic, crushed
2 potatoes, peeled and cubed
1 cup (250 mL) celery, minced
1 cup (250 mL) carrot, cubed
1 cup (250 mL) green beans, chopped
1 teaspoon (5 mL) salt
½ teaspoon (2 mL) freshly ground pepper
1 teaspoon (5 mL) dried oregano or 1 tablespoon (15 mL) fresh
1 teaspoon (5 mL) dried basil or 1 tablespoon (15 mL) fresh
1 cup (250 mL) zucchini, cubed
1 can (19 oz./540 mL) garbanzo beans
3 cups (750 mL) tomato juice
2½ cups (625 mL) water or vegetable stock
1 bottle (12 oz./341 mL) St. Ambroise Oatmeal Stout or Boréale Noire
3 tablespoons (45 mL) dry red wine
1 cup (250 mL) tomatoes, chopped
½ to ¾ cup (125 to 180 mL) dry macaroni
Parmesan cheese
Parsley, chopped

1. In pot, heat the oil and sauté the onion and garlic to translucency. Add the potatoes, celery, carrots, green beans and salt. Mix well. Add the pepper, oregano and basil. Mix again. Cover and cook for 15 minutes over low heat. Stir once or twice. Add the zucchini, cooked beans, sauce, stock, beer and wine and simmer for 30 minutes. Add tomatoes.

2. About 12 minutes before serving, bring to a boil. Add the pasta and boil gently until the noodles are tender.

3. Serve hot, topped with plenty of cheese and parsley.

Yellow Pea Soup with a Coup de Grisou

SERVES 8

Coup de grisou is the Walloon phrase for the explosion that occurs when methane gas from coal mines is ignited. The explosion in Le Cheval Blanc's Coup de Grisou is the buckwheat with which the beer is made. The herb additive is coriander, hints of which you can pick up on the nose and palate.

The traditional Quebec pea soup will be made with lard or salt pork. This is a full-bodied vegetarian alternative.

3 cups (750 mL) yellow split peas
Salt to taste
1 bay leaf
2 bottles (12 oz./341 mL each) Coup de Grisou
4 cups (1 L) water
1 large Spanish onion, diced
1 clove garlic, minced
3 medium carrots, diced
1 medium potato, diced
2 stalks celery, chopped
½ teaspoon (2 mL) dried thyme
Ground pepper to taste

1. Soak the peas overnight, eight hours minimum, with the salt and bay leaf in the beer and water. You may have to add water, a cup at a time, once or twice as the peas soak up the liquid.

2. Bring the peas to a boil, lower the heat and allow the peas to simmer for three hours.

3. Add the onion, garlic, carrots, potato, celery, thyme and pepper and simmer one more hour, or until all vegetables and peas are tender.

Roasted Squash, Carrot and Apple Soup

SERVES 8

Chef David Macgillivray, formerly of the Château Laurier Hotel in Ottawa, made a version of this soup several years ago with Unibroue's Blanche de Chambly. I adapted it slightly, cutting down on the water the chef had called for, and upping the curry to offset the sweetness of the maple syrup. I also added a Granny Smith apple for a little tartness. It looks like a lot of work, but it's really an easy soup to prepare and a hearty joy to eat.

2 medium onions, sliced
4 cloves garlic, chopped
3 large carrots, sliced
1 medium to large butternut squash, peeled, seeded and diced
1 large acorn squash, peeled, seeded and diced
½ cup (125 mL) olive oil
6 cups (1.5 L) water or vegetable broth
1 large Granny Smith apple, peeled, cored and diced
½ cup (125 mL) Blanche de Chambly
½ cup (125 mL) maple syrup
1 teaspoon (5 mL) ground cumin
1 teaspoon (5 mL) allspice
2 teaspoons (10 mL) curry powder
¼ teaspoon (1 mL) cinnamon
¼ teaspoon (1 mL) nutmeg
2 tablespoons (30 mL) fresh coriander, chopped
1 cup (250 mL) 35% heavy cream
Salt and pepper to taste

1. Preheat oven to the broiler setting.

2. On a baking sheet, place onion, garlic, carrot and squash. Drizzle with oil and place on the top rack of the oven. Broil until vegetables are lightly blackened.

3. Bring water to a boil in a large pot. Add apple and blackened vegetables. Return to boil, then reduce heat and simmer until vegetables are tender,

about 15 to 20 minutes. Reserve the liquid.

4. Purée the cooked vegetables and apple with some of the broth. Return purée and broth to the pot, whisking in the beer, syrup, spices, coriander and cream until desired consistency is reached. Heat through but do not boil. Season with salt and pepper to taste.

Strawberry-Cherry Cream Soup

SERVES 6

I especially enjoy surprising friends with this summer dessert soup. After they finished raving, you can let on that it was made with beer. Surprise surprise!

2 ample cups (500 mL plus) fresh strawberries
1 handful of cherries, 6 to 10, pitted
Juice of 2 oranges (about 7 tablespoons/105 mL)
1 cup (250 mL) 35% cream
½ cup (125 mL) sour cream
¼ teaspoon (1 mL) ground cinnamon
4 tablespoons (60 mL) Cheval Blanc Legendary Red
2 tablespoons (30 mL) Quelque Chose
2 tablespoons (30 mL) sugar, or to taste
4 strawberries, sliced thin for garnish

1. Purée the fruit and orange juice.

2. Blend in cream, cinnamon, beer and sugar.

3. Chill.

4. Garnish and serve.

Salads and Sides

Artichoke Strudel

MAKES 8

The big do at the Brewers Association of Canada in 1999 had a number of enticing dishes including "Mushroom Strudel With Yukon Gold Potatoes, Goat Cheese and Don de Dieu." Any longer and the title would have included how to prepare the dish. My version of the dish is made with artichokes, which are the real don de Dieu (gift of God) in this recipe.

2 tablespoons (30 mL) olive oil
3 cups (750 mL) artichoke hearts (or 2 14-ounce/398 mL cans, drained well and patted dry)
5 medium Yukon Gold potatoes, peeled and diced
2 leeks, white part only, diced
2 garlic cloves, minced
1 cup (250 mL) Don de Dieu
Salt and pepper to taste
1 tablespoon (15 mL) chives, freshly chopped or half that amount dried
⅔ cup (160 mL) goat cheese (herbed or plain)
Phyllo dough
¼ cup (60 mL) melted butter

1. Heat the olive oil in a large pot or skillet and cook the artichoke hearts, potatoes, leeks and garlic, stirring over medium heat, for about ten minutes or until leeks are tender.

2. Deglaze with beer. Add salt, pepper and chives and cook until beer has evaporated. Continue to cook until potatoes are almost cooked through.

3. Remove from heat. Add cheese and stir in to artichoke-potato mixture.

4. Preheat oven to 325° F.

5. Unfold a sheet of phyllo and brush with melted butter then repeat with another sheet. Cut the sheet in half widthwise. Spoon out the artichoke mixture near one end of the phyllo square. Roll like a cigar and fold over the ends.

6. Repeat #5 until all the mixture is used up. Should make eight "cigars" of artichoke strudel. Place on baking sheet and bake until golden brown, approximately 15 minutes.

———————

Blueberry Vinaigrette

Sweet and tangy like summer itself.

½ cup (125 mL) Folie Douce
⅓ cup (80 mL) olive oil
¼ cup (60 mL) balsamic vinegar
2 tablespoons (30 mL) wine vinegar
Fresh ground pepper to taste
¼ teaspoon (1 mL) salt
½ cup (125 mL) fresh blueberries

Mix together. Serve with mixed greens and a diced Granny Smith apple.

Chicken and Tomato Salsa

Salsa took over from ketchup as North America's No. 1 condiment in the late 1990s. It was about time. This is an extra-chunky version of the Mexican sauce that, combined with the chicken, can stand alone as a meal. Used alone, the salsa is fine with nacho chips.

For chicken
1 cup (250 mL) St. Ambroise Pale Ale
½ cup (125 mL) vegetable oil
½ cup (60 mL) apple cider vinegar
2 tablespoons (30 mL) Blanche de Chambly mustard (or Dijon)
Salt and coarsely ground pepper to taste
Green of one scallion, chopped
3 large boneless, chicken breasts, skinned

For salsa
½ cup (125 mL) coarsely chopped red onion
½ cup (125 mL) Mystique or light (low alcohol) apple cider
1 pound (500 grams) yellow and orange tomatoes, cored, seeded and chopped
1 red bell pepper, seeded and coarsely chopped
1 jalapeño pepper, seeded and minced
6 black olives, pitted and chopped
Green of 1 scallion, chopped
2 tablespoons (30 mL) fresh coriander, chopped
½ cup (125 mL) St. Ambroise Pale Ale

1. Combine the ingredients for the marinade and soak the chicken for two hours.

2. Combine the ingredients for the salsa and let soak in the beer.

3. Remove chicken from marinade and bake in a 350° F oven for 30 minutes.

4. When chicken is done, chop coarsely and mix with salsa.

Warm Salad of Smoked Duck, Quelque Chose Couscous and Napa Cabbage

SERVES 4

My first book on cooking with beer was Lucy Saunders' *Cooking With Beer*. It's a work of simplicity and art and I'm honored to have an original Saunders recipe in this book. Lucy has visited Montreal on several occasions and remains infatuated with Unibroue's cherry beer, around which this salad was made.

Couscous
¾ cup (180 mL) water
1 cup (250 mL) Quelque Chose
1 tablespoon (15 mL) butter
¾ cup (180 mL) couscous

Salad
5 ounces (150 mL) napa cabbage, slivered
3 ounces (85 mL) shredded carrots
½ cup (125 mL) celery, finely diced
2 tablespoons (30 mL) minced green scallion leaves
¼ cup (60 mL) dried cherries, chopped
2 tablespoons (30 mL) tangerine zest, minced
½ pound (250 grams) smoked duck breast (One half diced without the skin to toss with the couscous and the remaining half sliced against the grain of the breast meat into very, very thin slices to fan out on the plate. Try to get 12-16 slices.)
Salt and fresh ground pepper to taste

Quelque Chose dressing
¾ cup (180 mL) extra virgin olive oil
½ cup (125 mL) Quelque Chose
2 tablespoons (30 mL) balsamic vinegar
2 tablespoons (30 mL) cherry juice or melted cherry preserves
Pinch hot Chinese ginger powder
1 teaspoon (5 mL) kosher salt

1. Bring the water to a boil in a 2-quart saucepan. Pour in the beer and

butter, bring it back to a simmer, stir in the couscous and cover tightly. Turn off the heat and let sit for 12 to 15 minutes or until all the liquid is absorbed. Couscous should be tender and fluffy.

2. While couscous steeps, prepare salad ingredients.

3. Whisk together the dressing ingredients until an emulsion forms, use one-third of the dressing to toss with just the napa cabbage, reserve 3 tablespoons (45 mL) of the dressing to drizzle on duck slices, and use the remainder to dress the couscous vegetable mixture.

4. Mix the prepared couscous with two-thirds of the cabbage and all of the remaining vegetables/fruit/seasonings in the salad list. Add the warmed, finely diced duck breast. Stir in reserved dressing and season to taste.

5. Spread about ⅓ cup (80 mL) of the dressed napa cabbage on a plate, then mound one-quarter of the couscous mixture on top, and fan three to four of the thin slices of duck breast around the edges. Drizzle with a teaspoon (5 mL) of the reserved dressing.

St. Ambroise Glazed Carrots

SERVES 4 TO SIX

This is a variation of a classic and a favorite in our household; again it's the winning combination of sweetness and tang that makes this recipe so successful.

2 pounds (1 kg) carrots, peeled and sliced about ¼-inch thick
3 tablespoons (45 mL) unsalted butter
2 tablespoons (30 mL) St. Ambroise beer mustard
2 tablespoons (30 mL) brown sugar
Freshly chopped parsley

1. Boil carrots until cooked but not entirely tender. They should still maintain decent "raw" flavor.

2. Mix in remaining ingredients. Heat until butter is melted, sugar is dissolved. Mix so that mustard and parsley are evenly distributed.

McAuslan's Mixed Greens and Danish Blue Cheese Salad

SERVES 4 TO 6

E very year the Brewers Association of Canada holds a dinner during the course of its annual meeting. In 1998, the dinner featured a buffet in which courses were prepared with beer from the breweries of the members of the board of directors. Chef Rick Spensieri designed this recipe for McAuslan Brewery using St. Ambroise Pale Ale. It's a sweet, zippy dressing with the cheese adding a mellow dryness as a finishing note.

1 tablespoon (15 mL) St. Ambroise or Dijon mustard
¼ cup (60 mL) St. Ambroise Pale Ale
¼ cup (60 mL) balsamic vinegar
¾ cup (180 mL) olive oil
Salt and coarsely ground pepper to taste
1 tablespoon (15 mL) honey
Mixed greens (baby dandelion, baby arugula, endive, radicchio, chicory or other greens)
½ cup (125 mL) Danish blue cheese

1. Combine mustard, pale ale and vinegar in a bowl. While whisking, slowly add oil. Salt and pepper to taste. Whisk in honey.

2. Toss greens with dressing in a large serving bowl. Crumble cheese over salad and serve.

Potatoes with Rosemary
and the Raftman

This almost sounds like the title of a song by Bob Dylan. Either that or the name of a new rock group. Live, from Boise, it's The Raftman! There are no measurements here. It's completely adaptable to the number you're feeding, though an easy calculation is 1½ pounds (750 kg) potatoes for four people. You'll want to place the potatoes in a bowl and have enough beer and oil to cover.

Large potatoes
Raftman
Vegetable oil
Fresh rosemary, chopped
Green onions, chopped
Salt and pepper to taste

Cut potatoes in eighths lengthwise. Toss in a bowl with the remaining ingredients. The ratio of beer to oil is 2 to 1. Let sit a minimum of an hour. Heat oven to 350° F. Place the potatoes evenly on a tray and bake about an hour, or until the potatoes are tender. Can also be done in tinfoil on a grill.

———

Potatoes with Coriander and
Blanche de Chambly

Large potatoes
Blanche de Chambly
Vegetable oil
Fresh coriander, chopped
1 clove garlic, chopped
1 teaspoon (5 mL) chili powder
2 teaspoons (10 mL) lime juice
12 cherry tomatoes, halved

Same directions as in *Potatoes with Rosemary*, but don't add the tomatoes until the last 15 minutes or so of baking.

Red Potato and Fresh Bean Salad

SERVES 4 TO 6

Cheval Blanc's Coup de Grisou buckwheat beer adds a coriander hint to this salad, making an already savory side dish even more savory. The trick with the vegetables is not to overcook. Let the vegetables speak for themselves.

2 pounds (1 kg) small red potatoes
1 pound (500 kg) fresh green and waxed beans, trimmed
Fresh herbs, cut, to taste. Your choice here. I like basil, parsley, thyme and
mint, which gives the salad a special summery taste.
¼ cup (60 mL) olive oil
¼ cup (60 mL) Coup de Grisou
Zest of 1 lemon
Salt and pepper to taste

1. In separate pots, boil potatoes and beans in salted water until tender. Potatoes will take longer. Drain vegetables and place in large salad bowl.

2. Toss vegetables with oil, beer, lemon zest. Add salt and pepper. Serve at room temperature or chill until ready to use. (If you're going to do this, however, bring to room temperature before serving. Chilling can dull the flavors.)

Smoked Salmon Salad

I have a love-hate relationship with computers. I love the tool that has made my work so much easier. I love the speed at which I can access material and information. I hate crashing. I hate Internet spam. I hate the gap between rich and poor (technologically advanced and not) that increases at an ever-speeding rate and will continue no matter what Bill Gates says.

Several of Quebec's microbrewers are online with their own sites on the World Wide Web. Convenient links race readers to recipes using their beers, including this salad using Eau Bénite from Unibroue. For a complete list of beer-related Web sites, see the appendix.

1 cup (250 mL) Eau Bénite
16 snow peas
1 teaspoon (5 mL) Dijon mustard
¼ cup (60 mL) olive oil
1 tablespoon (15 mL) white wine vinegar
Salt and pepper to taste
½ cup (125 mL) smoked salmon, sliced thinly
1 tomato, seeded and diced
1 tablespoon (15 mL) parsley, chopped
Mixed lettuce leaves and mixed greens for four people

1. Bring the beer to a boil and reduce by three-quarters. Remove from heat and allow to cool.

2. Blanche the peas.

3. Mix together the mustard, oil, vinegar, salt and pepper and cooled beer. Add the peas, salmon, tomato and parsley.

4. Divide the lettuce and greens on four plates and place the salmon-vinaigrette mixture atop each.

Main Dishes

Viva Italia Spaghetti Sauce

A classic sauce and a classic beer combined for a memorable sauce.

Water for boiling
4½ pounds (2 kg) tomatoes
½ cup (125 mL) olive oil
2 large onions, diced
2 tablespoons (30 mL) fresh basil, coarsly chopped
1 teaspoon (5 mL) fresh oregano or half that dried
Salt and coarsely ground pepper to taste
1 bottle (12 oz./341 mL) Boréale Rousse
4 cloves garlic, chopped
½ cup (125 mL) parsley, chopped

1. Boil the water in a large pot. Score tomato bottoms with an X. Place tomatoes in boiling water for no more than a minute to loosen the skins. Reserve 2½ cups (625 mL) of the water for later use. Discard remaining water. Peel, seed and dice tomatoes.

2. In a pot, heat oil and cook onions over low heat for 20 minutes, until translucent. Add herbs, salt, pepper, and tomatoes and cook, stirring occasionally for 10 minutes.

3. Add reserved water and beer and simmer, uncovered, for three hours.

4. Add garlic and parsley and cook for 10 minutes.

5. Serve over favourite pasta.

Baya Cavaliere's Spaghetti Sauce

SERVES 4

Our friend Baya is a natural cook. Perhaps this comes from watching her mother, Maria; or it's in the vino she drank at home. This is her delicious sauce. It doesn't come any simpler than this. Makes enough sauce for one pound of pasta.

1 can (28 oz./796 mL) diced tomatoes
1 can (5½ oz./ (156 mL) tomato paste
Belle Gueule Rousse or U2
¼ cup (60 mL) extra virgin olive oil
4 or 5 garlic cloves, crushed
¼ cup (60 mL) fresh basil, chopped
Salt and freshly ground pepper, to taste

1. In a blender purée the tomatoes and paste with beer (one tomato-paste can-ful).

2. Heat the olive oil in a medium pot and cook the garlic for one minute. Don't let it brown. Add the tomato mixture and bring to a boil.

3. Reduce to a simmer, add the basil, salt and pepper and allow to simmer until thoroughly blended and thickened.

Variations: Mushrooms, olives, and sweet peppers can be added with the basil.

Spaghetti Sauce with Eggplant and Cinnamon

SERVES 4

Cinnamon has a tradition of spiciness that predates its North American use as a sweetener. In the Middle Ages cinnamon was used in stews, soups, custards, and fricassees. In this spaghetti sauce, cinnamon suggests a North African or Middle Eastern flavour. Paired with eggplant it could have been a sauce Marco Polo brought back from his trips to the East six hundred years ago.

⅓ cup (80 mL) olive oil
1 medium eggplant, in ½-inch cubes
1 tablespoon (15 mL) honey
2 tablespoons (30 mL) red wine vinegar
½ teaspoon (2 mL) ground cinnamon
Baya Cavaliere's Spaghetti Sauce

1. In a large skillet, heat the olive oil. Sauté the eggplant cubes until they are browned, then add them to Baya's sauce.

2. While the sauce simmers, dissolve the honey in the red wine vinegar. Add this to the sauce along with the cinnamon.

3. Continue to simmer until the flavors have completely blended.

Penne With Spring Vegetables and Pecans

This is my Crayola recipe, full of vibrant colors and different textures—deep greens, bursting yellows, bright reds—a canvas of *primavera* enjoyment for the palate.

1 pound (500 g) penne
1 pound (500 g) broccoli florets
2 small yellow zucchini, sliced thin
4 tablespoons (60 mL) olive oil
2 cloves garlic, minced
2 cups (500 mL) mushrooms, sliced
1 teaspoon (5 mL) each of fresh parsley, thyme, and basil, chopped
¼ cup (60 mL) Cheval Blanc Legendary Red
1 pound (500 g) cherry tomatoes, halved
2 ounces (60 g) pecan halves
Salt and freshly ground pepper to taste

1. Boil the pasta and drain when ready. In a separate pot, steam broccoli and zucchini.

2. In a large pan, heat olive oil and cook garlic, mushrooms, herbs and beer over high heat. Cook until the beer and olive oil have evaporated and the mushrooms have completely browned, about 5 minutes.

3. Add the broccoli, zucchini, tomatoes, and pecans to the mushroom mix. Salt and pepper. Cook for 2 minutes, stirring together.

4. Add vegetables to hot pasta.

Fettuccine and Shrimp with Chili Sauce

The heat, oh, the heat! La Fin du Monde gives this spicy sauce its body and, accompanying the meal, its respite as well. The heat in this dish doesn't come from the beer. It's the chipotle chilies. But La Fin du Monde does help bring these smoky jalapeños to life.

1 cup (250 mL) La Fin du Monde
4 chipotle chilies
2 tablespoons (30 mL) olive oil
1 cup (250 mL) onion, diced
4 cloves garlic, chopped
2 teaspoons (10 mL) ground cumin
1 tablespoon (15 mL) coriander, chopped
¼ cup (60 mL) apple cider vinegar
1 pound (500 g) fettuccine
¼ cup (60 mL) lime juice
2 tablespoons (30 mL) light or golden brown sugar
1½ pounds (750 g) tiny Matane shrimp

1. Warm ½ cup of the beer in a small pot with the dried chilies.

2. In a small skillet, heat the oil and sauté the onion until brown.

3. While the onion is cooking, drain (reserve beer) and chop the chilies into small pieces.

4. Add the garlic, cumin and coriander to the onion and cook another minute. Add the chilies, the beer they were reconstituted in, the remaining half cup of beer, and the vinegar. Mix well and remove from the heat.

5. Cook the fettuccine.

6. Purée the sauce until smooth in a blender or food processor. Pour into a medium saucepan and add the lime juice and brown sugar. Bring to a boil then reduce heat. Simmer for five minutes or until the liquid has reduced by half. Add the shrimp. Stir well so that the sauce coats each shrimp.

Cook for another five minutes over low heat or until shrimp are just cooked through.

7. Drain fettuccine and add shrimp sauce.

Note: Chipotles are dried, smoked jalapeños. If you can't find them in your market, substitute jalapeño peppers instead. There won't be anything to reconstitute so add all of the beer and the chopped jalapeños to the onion mixture at the same time as the vinegar. Then add a ½ teaspoon (2 mL) of liquid smoke with the shrimp to compensate for some of the smoked flavour missing from the regular jalapeño.

Apricot Chicken Pilaf With Almonds

SERVES 6

You're walking through an outdoor market in the Caucasus. A middle-aged woman in a floral print dress pushes forward with her hands together in prayerful fashion, an offering, a gift of freshness and sunshine. An apricot. You place your thumbs at the seam, exerting the tiniest amount of pressure so as not to bruise the flesh, and you halve the fruit. The tiniest drop of juice escapes onto your little finger and you bring it to your mouth.

You understand Eve.

But this is North America and somehow an apricot just doesn't taste the same here as it does in Tbilisi. This recipe, then, calls for dried apricots, which are available year-round, but come summer this should be made with the freshest you can find. Serve with a side dish of tabouleh, made with McAuslan's Apricot wheat ale.

1 pound (500 g) skinless, boneless chicken breast, cubed
1 teaspoon (5 mL) paprika
½ teaspoon (2 mL) ground cinnamon
1 pinch ground cardamom
2 tablespoons (30 mL) olive oil
1 large onion, diced
1 package (6.25 oz./185 mL) chicken-flavoured rice pilaf mix
2 cups (500 mL) McAuslan's Apricot wheat ale
½ cup (125 mL) chopped dried apricots
Zest of one orange
2 tablespoons (30 mL) fresh coriander, chopped
½ cup (125 mL) toasted walnuts, chopped

1. Mix the chicken with the spices. Heat the oil over medium heat in a large skillet. Cook the chicken until no longer pink, about 7 minutes. Remove from heat. With a slotted spoon set chicken aside.

2. In the remaining liquid, cook the onion until the liquid has evaporated and onion is translucent. Add pilaf mix with seasoning, beer, apricots, and orange zest. Bring to a boil. Cover, reduce heat and simmer about twelve minutes.

3. Add the coriander, walnuts, and chicken; cover and simmer for another twelve minutes or until liquid is absorbed.

Variation:
Substitute a game meat such as rabbit for the chicken; dried cherries for the apricots; and Unibroue's Quelque Chose for the beer.

St. Ambroise Chicken Curry

SERVES 8

The hoppy character of McAuslan's flagship beer, St. Ambroise Pale Ale, gives this mellow dish good balance.

3 tablespoons (45 mL) vegetable oil
3 large onions, chopped
¼ cup (60 mL) fresh ginger, peeled and finely chopped
3 garlic cloves, chopped
3 tablespoons (45 mL) curry powder
1 teaspoon (5 mL) ground cumin
¼ teaspoon (1 mL) ground cinnamon
2 tablespoons (30 mL) all-purpose flour
1 cup (250 mL) plain yogurt
3 tablespoons (45 mL) tomato paste
1 cup (250 mL) St. Ambroise Pale Ale
2 cups (500 mL) chicken broth
1 cup (250 mL) unsweetened applesauce
3 to 4 pounds (1.5 to 2 kilograms) skinless, boneless chicken breasts, cubed
1 package (10 oz./280 mL) frozen peas
½ cup (125 mL) sour cream
½ cup (125 mL) unsweetened coconut milk
Salt and freshly ground pepper, to taste
Fresh coriander

1. Heat oil in a large pot over medium-low heat. Sauté onions until golden. Add ginger and garlic and sauté another minute. Mix in the curry, cumin, and cinnamon, and cook for another minute.

2. Add the flour, followed by yogurt and tomato paste. Whisk until smooth. Add beer, broth and applesauce. Bring to a boil.

3. Reduce heat and simmer until sauce thickens, about 30 minutes. (If making a day ahead, cool, then cover and refrigerate. Bring back to a simmer before continuing the next day.)

4. Add chicken pieces and peas to the sauce. Cook until chicken is almost cooked through, 10 minutes. Add sour cream and coconut milk. Cook another 10 minutes until chicken is cooked through, but do not bring to a boil. Season with salt and pepper, to taste.

5. Serve in bowls, garnish with cilantro. Serve with steamed white rice and shelled roasted peanuts, or your favourite chutney.

Belle Gueule Chicken

Quebec microbrewers have taken advantage of many marketing devices to get their names imprinted on the consciousness of the beer-buying public—and their beers swirling around in people's glasses. A few of the microbrewers created a pamphlet that included some spectacular recipes. This Belle Gueule Chicken, a spicy, moist barbecued breast, is one of them.

2 tablespoons (30 mL) Belle Gueule
2 tablespoons (30mL) Asian chili paste
2 tablespoons (30 mL) old-fashioned or Dijon mustard
1 teaspoon (5 mL) melted honey
½ teaspoon (2 mL) tamari sauce, plus 2 tablespoons (30 mL)
1 bottle (12 oz./341 mL) Belle Gueule Rousse
2 cloves garlic, minced
1 teaspoon (5 mL) paprika
Salt and pepper to taste
4 boneless, skinned chicken breasts

1. In a bowl combine lager, chili paste, 1 tablespoon (30 mL) mustard, honey and ½ teaspoon (2 mL) tamari sauce. Refrigerate sauce.

2. In another bowl, combine beer, 1 tablespoon (30 mL) mustard, 2 tablespoons (30 mL) tamari sauce, garlic, paprika and salt and pepper. Place chicken in marinade and refrigerate for six hours, turning the chicken about halfway through.

3. Pat chicken breasts to remove some of the marinade. Place on the grill, brush on sauce and cover. Cook for 2 minutes. Turn the breasts, slather on sauce and continue cooking for 5 minutes with the grill cover closed. Turn the breasts once again and repeat with sauce. Cook for 2 additional minutes, covered.

Serve with rice and grilled vegetables or a salad.

Chicken Sauté

The sauté, or stir-fry, is an essential part of the home cook's repertoire. This particular recipe combines the best of the stir-fry—the high heat, almost flash-cooking of the meat and vegetables—with the more moderately paced, almost contemplative, making of a sauce.

½ cup (125 mL) oil
½ cup (125 mL) butter
1½ pounds (750 mL) chicken breast, cubed
1 onion, diced
6 small zucchini, cubed
1 red pepper, coarsely chopped
1 green pepper, coarsely chopped
1 cup (250 mL) mushrooms, quartered
1 cup (250 mL) snow peas
Salt and coarsely ground pepper, to taste
2 bottles (12 oz./341 mL each) Griffon Brown
1 cup (250 mL) 35% cream

1. In oil and butter, fry chicken until cubes have changed colour. Remove the chicken to a warm plate. Cook vegetables, one by one, in order of tenderness (most tender last).

2. Return chicken to the vegetable mixture, stir, season with salt and pepper to taste. Pour in beer. Simmer for 45 minutes.

3. Pour the bouillon into another pot, bring to a boil and reduce by half. Add the cream and cook until the sauce becomes smooth, about 20 minutes. Add to the chicken-vegetable mixture and bring to a boil. Season again with salt and pepper to taste.

Chambly Chicken with Tarragon

Blanche de Chambly is one of the most versatile of beers to cook with, as are many wheat-based ales. This is particularly true in this tarragon-tinged white sauce in which the slight coriander and malt flavours of the beer complement the anise hints of the tarragon. Tarragon is a popular herb to use with fowl, and Blanche de Chambly is a popular beer to cook and serve with fowl.

2 tablespoons (30 mL) unsalted butter, softened
Salt
Freshly ground pepper
2 tablespoons (30 mL) chopped fresh tarragon
Roasting chicken (3 pounds/1.5 kilograms)
1 cup (250 mL) Blanche de Chambly
2 tablespoons (30 mL) 35% cream

1. Preheat oven to 350° F. Mix the butter, salt and pepper and half the tarragon. Rub it into the cavity of the chicken. Truss the bird, and gently rub with the remaining butter mixture.

2. Roast the bird one hour and 15 minutes, or until its juice runs clear when you pierce the thickest part of the thigh. (Check after an hour has passed.)

3. Pour off the juice from the cavity. Remove the trussing strings. Set aside chicken. Reserve 2 tablespoons (25 mL) of fat. Scrape away remaining fat and brown bits. Place the chicken back in the roasting pan to keep warm. Heat the reserved fat and beer for 15 minutes to reduce. Stir in the remaining tarragon and cream. Season with salt and pepper to taste. Cook until the sauce has thickened. Carve and serve with the tarragon-cream sauce.

Chicken in Beer with Endives

SERVES 3 TO 4

Chef-owner James MacGuire of Passe-Partout in Montreal is in the restaurant/bakery business for love, wrote restaurant critic Byron Ayanoglu. "It's obvious. In every mouthful. In every sip. With every succeeding course. And during the aftermath, when happy but not stuffed, my stomach purrs with gratitude, as my palate sings from all the delightful tastes and flavours."

This is an adaptation of MacGuire's chicken and endive recipe, which calls for a black-and-tan of sorts: St. Ambroise's oatmeal stout and pale ale. Serve with boiled potatoes and steamed carrots.

1 3-pound (1.5 kg) chicken, or chicken breasts
Salt and pepper to taste
Butter
2 tablespoons (30 mL) vegetable oil
4 endives
1 large shallot, peeled and chopped
1 tablespoon (15 mL) flour
1 cup (250 mL) each St. Ambroise Oatmeal Stout,
St. Ambroise Pale Ale
1 cup (250 mL) brown veal stock
¼ pound (125 g) old-fashioned bacon
2 tablespoons (30 mL) brown sugar

1. Cut the chicken into 8 pieces or the breasts into ½-inch cubes. Season with salt and pepper. Brown the chicken in 2 tablespoons (30 mL) of butter and the vegetable oil. Remove before the cubes are cooked through and drain the pan.

2. Trim the endives and steam until almost tender.

3. Add the shallots to the pan the chicken was cooked in and sweat them in one tablespoon (15 mL) butter until transparent. Add flour and stir, then the beer and stock. Stir continuously until mixture comes to a boil. Lower heat and simmer for 10 minutes.

4. Cut the bacon into small strips and blanch.

5. Put the chicken pieces into the pan with the shallot sauce. Add the blanched bacon and simmer until cooked.

6. Squeeze the endives to remove excess water. Cut into halves. In another pan brown the endives in 1 tablespoon (15 mL) butter. Add ¼ cup (60 mL) of the sauce. Simmer the endives in the sauce until done. Taste the endive sauce, if bitter add brown sugar, then add to the chicken sauce. Salt and pepper to taste.

7. Arrange the endives around the chicken. Pour the sauce over the chicken.

Serve with boiled potatoes and carrots, garnished with chopped chives.

Lewinsky Chicken

SERVES 8

Denise remembered having a heavy-on-the-paprika chicken when she was growing up and called her mother for the recipe. It turned out to be Herb Chicken in Foil, once a popular menu item at Nicholson's Café in Manhattan. Denise's family called it Nicholson Chicken, but I could never remember the name and called it Lewinsky Chicken, a name that stuck. I adapted the original to accommodate beer, in this case, Unibroue's Raftman. Why Raftman? It's a whisky-malt-based beer, so it's got the requisite spiciness to balance the paprika. And there's that Whitewater thing...

½ cup (125 mL) butter, softened
2 tablespoons (30 mL) Hungarian paprika
4 teaspoons (20 mL) fresh thyme
2 teaspoons (10 mL) salt
1 teaspoon (5 mL) coarsely ground pepper
8 boneless, skinned chicken breasts
32 baby carrots
16 new potatoes
8 slices of bacon
Raftman or a smoked beer
2 lemons, quartered

1. Blend the butter, paprika, thyme, salt and pepper into a paste.

2. Rub the paste onto both sides of the chicken breasts.

3. Heat oven to 400° F. On 8 squares of aluminum foil, place 4 carrots and 2 potatoes on each.

4. Place a chicken breast on each of the potato-carrot combos and top with a strip of bacon.

5. Pour one tablespoon (5 mL) of Raftman over each breast.

6. Fold two sides of the foil down over the chicken in a double fold; fold the ends up in the same manner. Bake for one hour.

7. Open foil packages and squeeze the juice of one lemon quarter over each breast. Serve in the foil package.

"U"nique Omelet for One

B eer for breakfast. As if we're in U-niversity again.

2 eggs
2 teaspoons (10 mL) U
Salt and freshly ground black pepper to taste
1½ tablespoons (22 mL) unsalted butter

Filling
Fresh herbs
Grated cheese
Sautéed mushrooms

1. Beat eggs lightly with beer, then season with salt and pepper.

2. Melt butter in a skillet until it bubbles.

3. Add egg mixture. As egg begins to cook, shake the pan to spread the runny mixture equally over the cooked egg.

4. When the eggs are starting to set sprinkle the herbs, cheese and mushrooms over one-third of the egg. Fold the unfilled portion of the egg over the filling. Let cook about half a minute for cheese to melt. Serve hot.

Just about any combination of your favourites can be used as a filling. In savoury omelets, herbs such as chives, dill, chervil, tarragon, parsley, lemon balm, basil and sorrel are recommended. A dash of chili sauce or steak sauce would give the omelet a Mexican olé, as would guacamole, or slices of avocado with sour cream and scallions. Garnish with fine herbs. Omelets can be sweet, too, served at breakfast or at dessert. Substitute the Unibroue beer with its Quelque Chose or Folie Douce from Brasseurs de l'Anse and use fresh fruit and fresh whipped cream as a filling. Garnish with orange peel, cream, berries, ice cream. Any combo worth thinking up is worth trying.

Turkey Tourtière

MAKES 2 PIES / EACH SERVES 6 TO 8

The reveillon. Quebec's end-of-year holiday soirée that begins after midnight mass and lasts until the children wake to scamper down to the Christmas tree and uncover Santa's largesse. A feature at the reveillon is tourtière, or meat pie, which traditionally was made with ground beef and pork, sometimes potatoes depending on how poor a family was, or in the Saguenay-Lac Saint-Jean region, with moose. Though my family could afford to make meat pie that didn't call for a potato, my mother often added one anyway. It had a kind of "je me souviens" air about it, too. The darkened, post-solstice time of Christmas is occasion to remember—the kindness and good of the previous twelve months, the dead and the newborn, where we are and from where we come. So I toss in a potato. This tortière, however, is made with turkey, a non-red meat option.

Use your favourite pie crust recipe.

> 1½ pounds (750 mL) ground turkey
> 1 medium potato, diced
> 1 medium onion, finely diced
> 2 garlic cloves, minced
> ¼ teaspoon (1 mL) allspice
> Dash of ground cloves
> 2 teaspoons (10 mL) fresh thyme
> 1 cup (250 mL) turkey stuffing mix
> 1 egg
> 2 tablespoons (30 mL) Boréale Blonde or La Bolduc
> Pastry for 2 double-crust pies

1. In a large skillet over medium heat, cook the turkey, potato, onion, and garlic. Mix well and simmer for half an hour. Stir in the allspice, cloves and thyme, then remove from heat and cool.

2. Prepare the stuffing according to the box (or make your own, using croutons, herbs and spices). Set aside. When the meat is cool mix with stuffing.

3. Roll out pie pastry.

4. Preheat oven to 350° F.

5. Using a slotting spoon, fill two pie shells with mixture. Cover with top crust, crimp and slash (to make steam vents).

6. Beat egg and beer together well. Brush over each pie.

7. Bake for 35 minutes or until top crust is golden brown.

Waterzoie de Volaille à la Blanche

SERVES 6 TO 8

Chef Eric Lehousse learned about cooking with beer from his grandmother, a restaurateur in Belgium. Lehousse struck out on his own and ended up in Old Montreal as owner of Le Petit Moulinsart. His original Waterzoie called for Belgian Blanche de Bruge, but he suggests Blanche de Chambly if using Quebec beers.

2 scallions
2 medium onions
3 leeks, carefully washed
3 celery stalks
3 carrots
4 parsley stems (leafy heads are used later)
4 tablespoons (60 mL) butter
2 broiler chickens, 3 to 4 pounds (1.5 to 2 kg) each, cut up
3 to 5 bottles (12 oz./341 mL each) Blanche de Chambly
Salt and white pepper to taste
4 egg yolks
⅓ cup (80 mL) 35% cream
Juice of ½ lemon
1 tablespoon (15 mL) parsley leaf, chopped

1. Chop scallions, onions, leeks, celery, carrots and parsley stems finely. Melt half of the butter in large saucepan and stew vegetables for about 20 minutes.

2. Place chicken on top of vegetables, cover with beer, season with salt and pepper. Bring to boil, then simmer gently, covered, until the chicken is cooked.

3. As the chicken is cooking, beat yolks and cream together in a separate bowl. Add remaining butter, melted, to this mixture.

4. Remove chicken to warmed soup tureen. Keep warm. Pour a spoonful of hot liquid into the cream mixture, then gradually add it to the soup, whisking continuously on a gentle heat.

5. Season to taste with lemon juice. Add parsley leaf and pour over chicken in tureen.

6. Serve with boiled potatoes.

Aubergine and Pork with Belle Gueule Rousse

Serves 4 to 6

This is an adaptation of writer Dany Laferrière's favorite dish. When I asked Dany if there was a traditional Haitian dish that might be made with beer, he was quick to point out that Haiti, like other Caribbean and Latin American countries, is not exactly known for its beer. Dany is a generous man and this is a dish of generosity—serve ample portions.

1 tablespoon (15 mL) vegetable oil
2 large aubergines (eggplant), peeled and cubed
4 large carrots, peeled and sliced
4 green onions, sliced, including greens
1 clove garlic, minced
Salt and freshly ground pepper to taste
1½ pounds (600 grams) boneless pork, in 1-inch cubes
1 bottle (12 oz./341 mL) Belle Gueule Rousse
2 cups (500 mL) vegetable stock
1 can (5.5 ounces/156 mL) tomato paste
2 tablespoons (30 mL) fresh basil, chopped
2 tablespoons (30 mL) fresh coriander, chopped

1. Heat oil in large saucepan and cook aubergine cubes, stirring, about 15 minutes over medium heat. Add carrots, onions and garlic. Continue cooking, stirring continuously for another 5 minutes. Lower heat and cover, stirring occasionally.

2. Season the pork with the salt and pepper. Add the pork to a saucepan with the beer and stock and bring to a boil. Cook for 15 minutes.

3. Remove the pork with a slotted spoon and fry the pork about 5 minutes over medium heat to brown. Season again with salt and pepper, if desired. Add the tomato paste and stir well to coat the pieces of meat. Add basil. Cook 5 minutes then add the pork to the simmering vegetable mixture. The aubergines should be almost a purée by now.

4. Cook together, stirring, about 5 minutes before adding the coriander. Simmer 5 minutes and serve hot over steamed rice or egg noodles.

Paella de Matane

SERVES 8

A traditional rice-based Spanish dish that has variations around the world, the paella is also probably one of the most flexible meals to prepare. The substitutions, and therefore the possible combinations, are endless. Rabbit or chorizo sausage instead of the pork; zucchini and peppers instead of the eggplant and artichoke hearts; crustaceans instead of the shrimp. Try a completely vegetarian version by removing the pork, chicken and shrimp and loading up on eggplant, artichoke, zucchini, bell peppers, chili peppers, mushrooms and peas.

Even the beer, in this case Le Cheval Blanc's red wheat beer, Rescousse, can be replaced with stout.

1 large eggplant, chopped in half-inch (1.5 cm) cubes
Coarse salt
3 tablespoons (45 mL) olive oil
1¾ pounds (.75 kg) boneless pork, cut in half-inch (1.5 cm) cubes
4 pounds (2 kg) chicken thighs or drumsticks
Freshly ground pepper
2 large onions, diced
11 garlic cloves, minced
3 large tomatoes, chopped
2 bay leaves
2 jars (6oz./170 mL each) artichoke hearts, drained
2 pounds (1 kg) Matane shrimp
¼ teaspoon (1 mL) saffron threads
3½ cups (875 mL) chicken broth
1 bottle (12 oz./341 mL) Rescousse red wheat beer
2 teaspoons (10 mL) paprika
2½ cups (625 mL) long-grain rice

1. Place the cubed eggplant in a bowl and salt.

2. Heat 1 tablespoon (15 mL) of the olive oil in a large pot over medium heat. Cook the pork about 5 minutes, turning often, to brown. Add the chicken, season with salt and pepper and cook until chicken begins to brown. Turn chicken pieces and cook another 5 minutes. Remove chicken and pork to a bowl.

3. Cook the onions and 10 garlic cloves in the pot until the onions are translucent, 5-7 minutes. Add the tomatoes and bay leaves, eggplant and artichoke hearts. Cook over medium-low heat until tender but not completely cooked, 7-10 minutes.

4. Preheat the oven to 375° F.

5. In a bowl, toss the shrimp with 2 tablespoons (30 mL) olive oil, the remaining garlic clove and half the saffron.

6. Bring the broth, beer, paprika and the remaining saffron to a boil.

7. Brush a very large roasting pan with olive oil. Spread the uncooked rice evenly in the pan. Pour the vegetables and liquid over the rice. Push the pork and chicken into the vegetables and rice. Pour the boiled beer/broth mixture evenly over the rice. Cover with foil and bake for 40 minutes.

8. Remove from the oven, spread the shrimp evenly over the rice mixture. Season to taste with salt and pepper. Re-cover with foil and bake another 20 minutes until the shrimp is done, the rice is tender, and the liquid has been absorbed.

Pork Roll with Apples

This recipe was prepared by the Inter-Continental Hotel's executive chef, Christian Lévêque. It originally was made with Brasal Bock, but the recipe was too good to lose when the brewery closed. Griffin Brown is a wonderful alternative.

10 Yellow Delicious apples
1 lemon
½ cup (125 mL) butter
1 onion, diced
1 bottle (12 oz./341 mL) Griffon Brown
Oil
1¾ pounds (800 grams) pork loin*
Salt and coarsely ground pepper, to taste

1. Peel and core apples. Slice half of them in thin strips, quarter the remaining apples. Sprinkle lemon juice over the apples to prevent browning.

2. Cook all of the apples in the butter with the onion until the onions are translucent. Add half the beer. Continue to cook until the apples are soft but still retain their shape. Reserve the bouillon; refrigerate the quartered apples.

3. Unroll the pork onto an oiled cooking sheet or shallow pan. Season with salt and pepper. Place the apple slices on one end of the pork loin and roll it back up. Roast in 375° F oven for 15 minutes. Deglaze the pan with remaining beer and the bouillon. Turn the loin over carefully. Season again if necessary. Continue roasting for 15 minutes. Add quartered apples to pan and roast another 10 minutes.

* Have your butcher to cut the pork loin so that connected together, it can unroll like a roll of paper towels. Or use cutlets, which also works.

Sauerkraut and Sausage
with Royale de l'Anse

SERVES 2 TO 4

This is a make-ahead type of recipe. The cabbage sits in a salt bath a whole day before cooking. It is from Chef Christian Lévêque of the Inter-Continental Hotel, who has made cooking with beer one of his specialities.

9 cups (2.25 L) cabbage, finely chopped
⅓ cup (80 mL) coarse salt
5 tablespoons (75 mL) butter
1 muslin or cheesecloth bag containing:
8 juniper berries, 2 whole cloves, and 4 bay leaves
4 bottles (12 oz./341 mL each) Royale de l'Anse
⅔ cup (150 mL) canola oil
20 small new potatoes (grelot), washed
Salt and pepper to taste
2 Toulouse sausages
2 Strasbourg smoked sausages

1. Mix cabbage and salt together and keep in tightly sealed bowl in cool place for 24 hours, mixing occasionally.

2. Drain cabbage well and rinse. In a large pot over low heat, melt 2 tablespoons (30 mL) butter and sweat the cabbage, about 15 minutes, stirring. Place spice bag in pot and add 2 bottles of beer. Bring to a boil then simmer slowly for two hours.

3. About an hour and a fifteen minutes into the simmering, heat oil in a large skillet and brown the potatoes. When browned equally, add the sausages to brown.

4. Remove potatoes and sausages to a casserole dish, add remaining two bottles of beer, salt and pepper to taste, and bake at 350° F for 35 minutes.

5. Then add to cabbage and simmer together for 5 to 10 minutes. Remove spice bag.

Veal Medallions with Boréale Cuivrée

This recipe calls for Boréale Cuivrée, the strong beer from Brasseurs du Nord, along with cream, cheese and flour in a sauce that typifies French cuisine.

1½ pounds (750 g) veal fillet
Salt and pepper to taste
1 tablespoon (15 mL) butter
¼ cup (60 mL) scallions, chopped
1 bay leaf
1 tablespoon (15 mL) parsley, chopped
1 sprig thyme
1 cup (250 mL) Boréale Cuivrée or strong ale
1 cup (250 mL) vegetable broth
¼ cup (60 mL) 35% cream
1 cup (250 mL) goat cheese (chèvre), diced
1 teaspoon (5 mL) Dijon mustard
1 tablespoon (15 mL) all-purpose flour

1. Cut veal fillet into medallions and season with salt and pepper.

2. Heat butter in a frying pan and brown veal on both sides, maintaining a slight pinkness inside. Remove from pan and set aside.

3. Brown the scallions and fresh herbs in the pan juices for three minutes.

4. Pour beer, broth, and cream into pan; add cheese and mustard. Cook until liquid is reduced by half.

5. Add flour. Stir continuously until sauce thickens.

6. Place medallions on serving platter and nap with the sauce. Serve alongside your favourite vegetables.

Trois Pistoles Basting Sauce for Steak

The sweetness in the Trois Pistoles strong ale picks up on the sugar in the basting sauce to offset the heat in the mustard, Tabasco and Worcestershire combo for an interesting, mildly piquant steak sauce.

2 tablespoons (30 mL) wine vinegar
1 tablespoon (15 mL) sugar
2 tablespoons (30 mL) water
2 teaspoons (10 mL) Dijon mustard
Freshly ground pepper and salt to taste
¼ teaspoon (1 mL) hot sauce, such as Tabasco
½ lemon, thickly sliced
Juice from one end slice of lemon
1 small onion, sliced
1 tablespoon (15 mL) Worcestershire sauce
¼ cup (60 mL) Trois Pistoles or strong ale
2 tablespoons (30 mL) butter

1. In a skillet, combine: vinegar, sugar, water, mustard, salt and pepper, hot sauce, lemon, lemon juice and onion. Simmer on low heat about 15 minutes.

2. Add Worcestershire sauce, beer and butter and bring to boil.

3. Strain.

4. Use as a basting sauce for slowly barbecued steak.

Carbonnade à la Flamande

Serves 6 to 8

This dish, originating in Flanders, the region of northern France, Belgium and parts of the Netherlands, is perhaps the most well-known of beer dishes. It is distinctive, delicate in flavour, yet hearty. It is a simple dish to prepare, but one that requires patience, too. Any rushing, in the preparation of either the onions or the beef, will leave you with a bitter, gray dish.

Serve a brown ale or strong ale alongside the carbonnade.

Traditionally, one has boiled new potatoes, but I prepared this with egg noodles and Asparagus à la Flamande, made by cooking asparagus in a pot of boiling salted water. Serve the spears with melted butter, garnished with sieved hard-boiled egg yolks, and chopped fresh parsley.

8 to 10 slices of bacon, cut in one-half inch (1.5 cm) lengths
3 tablespoons (45 mL) vegetable oil
1¾ pound (800 grams) onions, sliced
1¾ pound (800 grams) stewing beef,
or top round cut into half-inch (1.5 cm) cubes
2 tablespoons (30 mL) flour
1 cup (250 mL) beef stock
1 bottle (12 oz./341 mL) Trois Pistoles
1 garlic clove, minced
½ teaspoon (2 mL) salt
1 bay leaf
1 sprig of thyme
1 tablespoon (15 mL) parsley, plus parsley for garnish
1 tablespoon (15 mL) brown sugar
1 teaspoon (5 mL) red wine vinegar

1. Blanch the bacon in boiling water. Drain then pat dry. In a frying pan, heat 1 tablespoon (15 mL) of the oil over medium heat and fry the bacon. Remove to a paper towel-lined plate, reserve the fat in the frying pan.

2. While the bacon is frying, heat the remaining oil in another frying pan over medium-low heat, and cook the onions, covered, for 20 minutes.

They must not be allowed to brown or burn, which will embitter the onions.

3. Heat the fat reserved in the first frying pan. Brown the beef cubes, five to six pieces at a time, until all sides are browned. Cooking more than a half-dozen pieces at a time will only lower the temperature of the pan, resulting in gray, dried-out pieces of meat. As each set of beef cubes are browned, remove them to a large casserole.

4. Preheat the oven to 325 degrees.

5. When all the meat is browned and in the casserole, remove the pan from the heat and add 1 tablespoon (15 mL) flour to the fat. Stir the fat and flour together to make a roux, or paste, and return to cook over low heat, stirring constantly. When the roux is a dark, nut brown, add the stock and ½ cup (125 mL) of the beer. Whisk together until the sauce is thick (you may have to add the remaining tablespoon of flour). Stir in the garlic, salt, bay leaf, thyme, 1 tablespoon (15 mL) parsley, brown sugar and vinegar. Mix together then remove from heat.

6. Pour onions over meat in the casserole, then pour the sauce over the onions and beef. The sauce should cover the onions and meat. Not to worry if it doesn't. Just add more beer.

7. Bake for one hour until beef is tender. Taste about one-third of the way through and add salt if needed.

8. Serve with parsley garnish, alongside Asparagus à la Flamande and egg noodles.

Red Line Chili

Chili is another of those traditional beer recipes. Everyone, it seems, has a recipe for chili. Mine I have adapted over a couple of years, borrowing from this one and that one, until I found something I like. It's kind of the way a winning hockey team is put together, I guess. A wing from here, a goaltender from there, someone who can shoot, and there you go: a team that scores.

I call this Red Line Chili because of its heat and in honour of Red Fisher, the dean of hockey writing in Canada, a sports writer and editor at *The Gazette* in Montreal, whose Saturday-morning column is called The Red Line.

Chili aficionados will find a couple of oddities, perhaps, in this chili. One is that I call for a certain amount of sweetness. This comes in the form of the cocoa powder, the cinnamon and the roasted red pepper sauce. As in my barbecue sauce, I like a balance of tanginess and sweetness and, in the chili, smokiness and the requisite sizzle. The cocoa powder idea I borrowed from John Balzar of the *Los Angeles Times*.

1 pound (500 g) ground beef
1 pound (500 g) ground pork
3 cups (750 mL) vegetable stock
1 tablespoon (15 mL) cumin
1 teaspoon (5 mL) Hungarian paprika
1 teaspoon (5 mL) white pepper
1 teaspoon (5 mL) dry mustard
2 teaspoons (10 mL) cayenne
½ tablespoon (8 mL) chili powder
1 tablespoon (15 mL) crushed dry bay leaves
1 can (5½ oz./156 mL) tomato paste
1 can (24 oz./680 mL) tomato sauce
2 cans (19 oz./540 mL each) black beans
1 bottle (12 oz./341 mL) bottle Loch Ness or McAuslan Scotch ale
2 tablespoons (30 mL) roasted red pepper cooking sauce (optional)
2 small red chili peppers, minced
2 cups (500 mL) onions, chopped coarsely
2 cloves garlic, minced

10 crisp bacon slices, cut in pieces
2 teaspoon (10 mL) cocoa powder
1 cinnamon stick
1 teaspoon (5 mL) liquid smoke
Parmesan cheese, grated, optional
Fresh chopped parsley, optional

1. In a skillet, brown meats over medium heat.

2. In a pot bring to a simmer the vegetable stock, cumin, paprika, white pepper, mustard, cayenne, chili powder and bay leaves, tomato paste and sauce, beans, beer and red pepper sauce.

3. Transfer browned meat to simmering sauce with a slotted spoon. Sauté the red chili peppers, onion and garlic until translucent. Add to sauce along with bacon, cocoa powder and cinnamon stick. Simmer for one hour.

4. Remove cinnamon stick, add liquid smoke and simmer for another hour. Serve in bowls, garnished with cheese and parsley, and with hunks of bread, or over noodles or rice.

Mike's Chocolate Chili

My friend ande co-worker, Michael Shenker, says "Every time I make this chili,it comes out a little different. But there are two constants: chocolate and beer. The chocolate is there because I love spicy Mexican dishes that use it. The amber beer gives the chili a nice taste and a little extra bite. Besides, there's nothing more fun than dumping a bottle of beer into a large pot of food and watching it foam up."

Agreed.

2 pounds (1 kg) dry, small red kidney beans
Cold water
4 tablespoons (60 mL) vegetable oil
2 large onions, cut in large chunks
5 large or 8 medium cloves garlic, crushed
1 can (28 oz./796 mL) crushed tomatoes
2 tablespoons (30 mL) plus 1 teaspoon (5 mL) ground cumin
2 bottles (12 oz./341 mL each) Boréale Rousse or amber beer
1½ teaspoons (7 mL) cayenne pepper
2½ teaspoons (12 mL) salt
1 square (1 oz./28 g) unsweetened chocolate
1 square (1 oz./28 g) semi-sweet chocolate
3 large carrots, coarsely chopped
3 medium zucchini, coarsely chopped
4 red bell peppers, seeded and coarsely chopped
2 green bell peppers, seeded and coarsely chopped
4 cups (1 L) frozen corn kernels
Juice of 1 lime
Chopped fresh coriander
Plain yogurt (optional)

1. Soak the beans in a large pot of cold water overnight or for at least eight hours.

2. In another large pot, heat oil over medium heat and sauté onions until soft. Add garlic and continue to sauté for a few minutes. Discard all but

about 1 cup (250 mL) of the bean soaking liquid and add beans and remaining liquid to the onions.

3. Add tomatoes, cumin and one bottle of the beer. Heat until mixture simmers; add cayenne and simmer very gently for 1½ to 2 hours, or until the beans are almost tender.

4. Add the second bottle of beer and the carrots and continue simmering for about 15 minutes.

5. Add the two squares of chocolate, salt, zucchini, red and green peppers. When the vegetables are cooked to the crisp-tender stage, add the corn, heat and serve, topped with lime juice, coriander and yogurt.

Lamb Chili

SERVES 8 TO 10

I met Johanna Burkhard when she wrote the "What's Cooking?" column for *The Gazette* newspaper in Montreal. I was often her editor. It was always a treat to call her with questions and chat about recipes. Johanna is also the author of *The Comfort Food Cookbook*.

Johanna originally concocted this recipe for a novel I had written that was set in Yorkshire, England, where lamb is plentiful. In using canned beans and tomatoes, it cuts a few corners because the main character in the novel is a bit short on cash. If you're using dried beans make sure to soak them overnight in water first. So here is the recipe, adapted to accommodate the beer. If you can't find Griffon Brown, Newcastle—that Yorkshire stalwart—would do just fine.

½ cup (125 mL) Griffon Brown
2 chipotle chilis
1 tablespoon (15 mL) olive oil
1 onion, diced
2 cloves garlic, minced
1 sweet red pepper, diced

1 can (28 oz./796 mL) tomatoes, drained and chopped
1 tablespoon (15 mL) chili powder
1 teaspoon (5 mL) each ground cumin and oregano
1 pound (500 g) lean ground lamb
1 can (19 oz./540 mL) kidney beans, drained and rinsed
Salt and ground pepper to taste
¼ cup (60 mL) chopped fresh coriander

1. Bring beer to a boil. Shut off heat, add chilis and allow to reconstitute.

2. In a medium-sized pot, over medium-high heat, warm oil then sweat onion, garlic and pepper until vegetables are softened; about five minutes. Chop chilis and add to vegetables along with tomatoes, chili powder, cumin and herbs. Reduce heat to simmer.

3. In a skillet brown the lamb in the beer.

4. Add the lamb to the pot, cover and simmer for 15 minutes. Add the kidney beans, salt and pepper to taste and cook for five minutes.

5. Ladle into bowls and sprinkle with coriander.

Oven-Poached Salmon With Herbs

Serves 2

Poaching is a great way to keep fish moist. Stout is a great beer to cook with and is the perfect accompaniment to certain seafoods like salmon, and oysters. This recipe also works well with trout.

1 cup (250 mL) Boréale Noire
½ teaspoon (2 mL) basil
¼ teaspoon (1 mL) each of thyme and dill
1 pound (500 grams) Atlantic salmon fillet
1 lemon, sliced
1 small onion, sliced
A dozen or so capers
Coarse salt
Freshly ground pepper

1. Preheat oven to 375° F. Bring the beer and herbs almost to the boiling point.

2. Place the salmon in aluminum foil with lemon and onion slices and capers. Salt and pepper to taste. Fold up sides and ends of foil. Pour the hot liquid over the salmon.

3. Bake at 375° F for 35 minutes.

Ephemeral Salmon Pie

SERVES 6

My mother used to make a variation on shepherd's pie that was canned salmon, mashed potatoes, and a dash of paprika. For Fridays during Lent, it was quite the treat.

This salmon pie is not my mother's—it has a crust and a half-cup of beer. Mom probably wouldn't have done that, considering we ate salmon during Lent. Had she done so, we would have been following a tradition going back 500 years. The monks and abbots of the medieval ages drank beer, nutritious and filling, to sustain them during the forty-day fasting period.

1 pound (500 g) boneless salmon fillet
½ cup (125 mL) Ephémère original
1 bay leaf
Salt and coarsely ground pepper to taste
2 tablespoons (30 mL) butter
1 onion, finely chopped
1 stalk celery, finely chopped
3 medium potatoes, peeled and diced
2 tablespoons (30 mL) all-purpose flour
1 cup (250 mL) whole milk
1 tablespoon (15 mL) fresh dill, chopped
Single-crust 9-inch pie pastry

1. Preheat oven to 400° F. Place salmon in a shallow baking dish. Add beer and bay leaf and season with salt and pepper. Bake for 15 minutes or until salmon flakes easily, and let cool. Flake the salmon. Reserve the liquid.

2. Melt butter in a saucepan over medium heat. Add onion, celery and potatoes and cook, stirring, for five minutes, or until vegetables are soft.

3. Sprinkle flour over the vegetables, add milk and reserved liquid. Cook two to three minutes until sauce boils and thickens. Stir in salmon and dill, season with salt and pepper. Mix well. Remove from heat and cool.

4. Butter a 9-inch pie plate. Spread salmon mixture evenly into the pie

plate and cover with layer of pastry. Crimp the edges and cut steam vents. Bake in oven at 425° F for 20-25 minutes, until pastry is lightly browned and filling bubbles.

———

Grilled Yellow Tuna Teriyaki

SERVES 2 TO 3

Cooking time here is almost nothing, which makes this an anyday kind of meal. Prepare the teriyaki marinade in the morning, let the tuna—and accompanying vegetables or shiitake mushrooms, for example—marinate for the day. Fire up the grill when you get home from work. Bingo.

½ cup (125 mL) St. Ambroise Pale Ale
½ cup (125 mL) freshly squeezed orange juice
¼ cup (60 mL) soy sauce
¼ cup (60 mL) canola oil
2 teaspoons (10 mL) sesame seeds
2 cloves garlic, crushed
1 teaspoon (5 mL) freshly grated ginger
1 tablespoon (15 mL) brown sugar
1 pound (500 g) yellow tuna (3 or 4 steaks)

Blend marinade ingredients together. Pour over tuna and marinate in the refrigerator for 6 hours or more. Preheat grill, remove tuna from marinade, then grill for 5 minutes each side.

Scallops with Couscous

L a Maudite permeates the scallops and the soft vegetables and combines with the spices and the couscous, the way the Mediterranean defines the lands and peoples that surround it.

⅓ cup (80 mL) olive oil
3 medium onions, diced
8 garlic cloves, crushed
3 tablespoons (45 mL) tomato paste
1½ tablespoons (22 mL) ground cumin
1 tablespoon (15 mL) paprika
4 bottles (12 oz./341 mL each) Maudite
2 whole jalapeño peppers
1 teaspoon (5 mL) coarse salt
2 pounds (1 kg) baking potatoes (Russet),
peeled, halved and cut into wedges
1 large turnip, peeled and cut in half-inch (1.5 cm) sticks
1 large red bell pepper, seeded, cut in strips
1 can (19-ounce/580 mL) chickpeas, drained
2 pounds (1 kg) scallops
Salt and coarse ground pepper to taste
2 cups (500 mL) couscous

1. Heat oil in large pot over medium heat. Sauté onions and garlic until translucent. Add tomato paste, cumin, and paprika. Stir well and cook about one minute.

2. Add beer and jalapeño peppers and bring to a boil. Reduce heat, cover and simmer for 15 minutes.

3. Add salt and potatoes. Simmer for 10 minutes.

4. Add turnip, pepper and chickpeas. Simmer for 10 minutes.

5. Add scallops. Season with salt and pepper to taste. Cook until scallops and vegetables are cooked through, soft but maintaining shape, about 10

minutes. Discard peppers, if desired.

6. Place couscous in a bowl. Add 2½ cups (625 mL) of the cooking liquid to couscous. Cover and let couscous absorb the liquid, about 5 minutes.

7. Mound couscous on a large platter. Top with scallops and surround with vegetables.

Seafood Cassoulet

Serves 6 to 8

A traditional cassoulet is a bean and pork dish from the Languedoc region of France. "Cassoulet" comes from the word *cassole*, the glazed earthenware in which the dish was normally prepared. This rich stew, a recipe from Chef Christian Lévêque, is a Quebec marine version—no beans, however—but as hearty as the stout with which it's made.

White sauce
½ cup (125 mL) butter
½ cup (125 mL) flour

Stew
2 medium onions, diced
1 tablespoon (15mL) butter
1 cup (250 mL) scallops
Salt
4 bottles (12 oz./341 mL each) Boréale Noire
9 pounds (4 kg) mussels, washed (discard open ones)
1 tablespoon (15 mL) parsley, chopped
Salt and coarsely ground pepper, to taste
2 cups (500 mL) mushrooms
1¼ cups (310 mL) Matane shrimp
Plain yogurt

1. Prepare the white sauce. Melt butter in a saucepan incorporating the

flour gradually. Cook at lowest temperature 10 minutes. Chill.

2. Sweat one of the diced onions in butter. Add the scallops, and salt lightly. Add one bottle of beer and bring to a boil for four minutes. Remove the scallops to a dish and conserve the bouillon.

3. Sweat the remaining onion in butter with parsley. Add mussels, salt and pepper to taste. Pour in remaining bottles of beer. Bring to a boil to open up mussels. Stir once or twice to make sure all mussels have opened. Remove the mussels, discarding unopened ones, add the bouillon from the scallops to this conserved bouillon and bring to a boil. While it comes to a boil, remove the mussels from their shells.

4. Add some of the boiled bouillon to the chilled white sauce. Whisk until you've got a smooth liquid. Combine all of the bouillon with the white sauce. Mix with all the seafood and mushrooms. Heat almost to boiling point.

5. Remove from heat, add yogurt to taste and mix well. The yogurt will lessen the bitterness of the beer.

———

Stuffed Salmon with Stout

SERVES 6 TO 8

Michael Lomonaco, executive chef of Windows on the World, had an optician's appointment that kept him away from his restaurant the morning of September 11, 2001. Almost all his staff perished. I thank Michael for the use of it, and thank God Michael's still around to enjoy it.

1 baguette, cut into ½ inch (1.25 cm) cubes
1 cup (250 mL) Boréale Noire or stout
½ cup (125 mL) olive oil
6 shallots, chopped
1 large leek, white part only, washed and diced
1 cup (250 mL) carrots, chopped finely
Coarse salt and freshly ground black pepper to taste

3 cups (750 mL) spinach leaves, patted dry
4 large cloves of garlic, minced
2 tablespoons (30 mL) fresh thyme (or half that amount dry)
2 tablespoons (30 mL) fresh tarragon (or half that amount dry)
7 pounds (3 kg) fresh Atlantic salmon*

1. Soak the bread in half of the beer.

2. Heat 2 tablespoons (30 mL) of the oil for about a minute over medium heat in a large saucepan. Add the shallots, leek and carrots, then season with salt and pepper to taste. Cook for just under 10 minutes, until vegetables are soft. Remove and reserve in a bowl.

3. Heat another 2 tablespoons (30 mL) of oil. Cook the spinach until wilted.

4. Add the beer and cooked vegetables to the spinach, and cook for another minute. Add the garlic and herbs; cook for 2 more minutes. Add the beer-moistened bread, mix thoroughly. Remove to a platter or bowl and refrigerate.

5. Preheat oven to 425° F.

6. Pour 3 tablespoons (45 mL) of oil in a large roasting pan and place the salmon in the pan. Rub salt and pepper in the cavity and then stuff with the vegetable stuffing mix. Tie with kitchen cord to keep the stuffing from coming out. Spread the remaining olive oil over salmon. Roast for 50 minutes until the fish is firm and the stuffing piping hot.

* Have your fishmonger remove the scales, gut it and butterfly it. You can keep the head on or off; on makes a nicer, more restaurant-like presentation. Or you can save the head to make stock.

Variation
Rice and Mushroom Stuffing

2 tablespoons (30 mL) butter
¾ cup (180 mL) sliced mushrooms
1 large carrot, diced
1 teaspoon (5 mL) basil, chopped
1 teaspoon (5 mL) fresh thyme

Zest of 2 lemons
¾ cup (180 mL) wheat beer
2 cups (500 mL) instant rice
1 cup (250 mL) chopped green onion, green included

1. Melt the butter in a skillet and sauté the mushrooms and carrot about five minutes. Add the basil and thyme, lemon zest and beer. Bring to a boil and add the rice and green onion. Cover, remove from heat, and allow rice to stand for five minutes.

2. Prepare the salmon as above, then stuff with rice and mushroom mixture.

————

Trout Roulade with Asparagus

SERVES 4

We are blessed with five senses. In cooking and eating, smell and taste are paramount. But we'd be wrong to limit it to just those two. Beer judges will tell you hearing is important. When opening a bottle of beer, you want to hear the rush of gas escaping. It's a clue to the carbonation of the beer inside. And touch. How can you tell the ripeness of a cantaloupe without smelling and squeezing it?

A well-prepared and visually attractive dish increases a diner's anticipation of a meal. This adaptation of the Trout Roulade with Asparagus was originally prepared for McAuslan Brewery by René Juneau. The long, forest-green stems of asparagus, the sunset-rose of the trout, and the buttery yellow of the beer-cream sauce, tastes terrific and looks wonderful, too. My mouth is watering just writing about it.

16 medium-length asparagus spears
7 ounces (210 g) smoked trout or smoked salmon
1 egg white
Garlic and freshly ground pepper, to taste
3 tablespoons (45 mL), plus ½ cup (125 mL) 35% cream
4 trout fillets, 6-7 ounces (200-225 g) each
2 tablespoons (30 mL) plus ½ cup (125 mL) Griffon Brown

1 tablespoon (15 mL) white wine vinegar
1 shallot, finely chopped
½ cup (125 mL) butter at room temperature
Salt and freshly ground pepper to taste

1. Preheat oven to 350° F.

2. Blanch the asparagus.

3. In a blender, purée the smoked trout, egg white, garlic and pepper. Add 3 tablespoons (45 mL) cream and mix for 2 minutes to achieve a fine puree.

4. Spread the purée on the fillets. Place four spears of asparagus on each fillet, crosswise, and roll. Place each roulade on a lightly greased baking sheet, sprinkle with 2 tablespoons of beer, and bake in the oven for 18 to 20 minutes.

5. In a saucepan, cook the remaining beer, vinegar and shallot until there's virtually no liquid left. Add the cream, bring to a boil then lower the heat and reduce by two-thirds.

6. Remove from heat, add the butter gradually, stirring constantly. Salt and pepper to taste.

Serve with a rice and spring vegetable mixture. Garnish with capers, sprigs of dill and parsley.

Grilled Antilles-Style Swordfish
(Espadon grillé aux parfums des Antilles)

Cuba, Puerto Rico, Jamaica and the Hispaniola island comprising the Dominican Republic and Haiti are also known as the Greater Antilles. The Lesser Antilles is the chain of numerous small islands to the southeast of Puerto Rico, including Martinique and Saint Vincent and the Grenadines. The Caribbean Sea that surrounds these islands is rich in "fruits de mer," such as marlin and swordfish—images of Hemingway's *The Old Man and the Sea.*

This is an adaptation of a recipe by Chef Ronald Marcotte using Titanic, a strong ale from Le Cheval Blanc. He called for exotic fruits and grilled sweet peppers as garnishes. I would suggest a side of yucca (a tuber native to the Antilles), rice, grilled peppers, pomegranates, ripe granadilla passionfruit.

1 bottle (12 oz./341 mL) Titanic
½ cup (125 mL) pineapple juice
¼ cup (60 mL) olive oil
2 tablespoons (30 mL) herbes de Provence
1 teaspoon (5 mL) freshly ground ginger
1 teaspoon (5 mL) paprika
1 teaspoon (5 mL) red pepper flakes, or to taste
1 scallion, chopped
Zest of one lemon
Zest of one lime
Salt and freshly ground pepper to taste
2 swordfish steaks (enough for four people)

1. Bring the beer and pineapple juice to a boil. Lower the heat and simmer until the liquid is reduced by three-quarters. Refrigerate.

2. Mix together the olive oil, herbes de Provence, ginger, paprika, pepper, scallion, zests, salt and pepper. Add to the beer.

3. Marinate the fish in the herb-beer mixture for two to three hours. Grill five to eight minutes each side, depending on thickness.

From the Bread Oven
and Griddle

Cranberry Bread

Southeastern Massachusetts along the coast heading toward Cape Cod (not far from where I lived for several years) is one big bog—the source of most of the cranberries produced in the United States, and the inspiration for Samuel Adams' Cranberry Wheat beer.

Quebec has a fine tradition of cranberry-growing, as well, much of it produced near the Nicolet River where I spent several weeks' worth of summer splashing near my grandfather's chalet. And wouldn't you know, Le Cheval Blanc makes a cranberry beer, too, for Christmas, called Le Snoreau.

The bread is perfect for breakfast, with an apricot spread, or warmed up with some melting butter.

2⅓ cups (580 mL) all-purpose flour
2 teaspoons (10 mL) baking powder
½ teaspoon (2 mL) salt
⅓ cup (80 mL) sweet butter, softened
⅔ cup (160 mL) sugar
2 large eggs
½ cup (125 mL) Snoreau
⅔ cup (160 mL) apricot spread
1 cup (250 mL) fresh cranberries

1. Preheat the oven to 375° F degrees.

2. Sift together the flour, baking powder, and salt.

3. In a separate bowl, cream the butter and sugar using an electric mixer. Beat in the eggs one at a time. Mix in the beer. Mix in the apricot spread with a wooden spoon. Add the flour mixture and blend together. Add the cranberries.

4. Oil and flour a 9-inch loaf pan. Pour in the mixture and bake for about an hour, or until a tester comes out clean. Cool the loaf for about 10 minutes, then turn out on a rack to cool completely.

Blonde Banana Bread

This recipe was adapted from a handwritten copy of an old banana bread recipe Denise found in a bread book. She added beer and dropped nuts from the list of ingredients mostly because I've never been nuts about nuts in my bread.

½ cup (125 mL) butter
1 cup (250 mL) sugar
2 eggs, lightly beaten
1 cup (250 mL) ripe banana, mashed
1 cup (250 mL) all-purpose flour, unsifted
1 cup (250 mL) whole wheat flour, unsifted
½ teaspoon (2 mL) salt
1 teaspoon (5 mL) baking soda
⅓ cup (80 mL) Tourmente, heated but not boiled

1. Preheat oven to 325° F.

2. Melt the butter and blend in sugar. Mix in the beaten eggs and mashed banana, blending until smooth.

3. In a bowl, stir together the two flours, salt and baking soda until thoroughly blended. Add the dry ingredients alternately with the hot beer.

4. Spoon the batter into an oiled loaf pan. Bake in the oven for about an hour, or until bread begins to pull away from the sides of the pan and a wooden skewer or toothpick inserted in the centre comes out clean.

5. Cool in the pan for ten minutes before turning it out to cool completely.

French Toast

Malt extract is available wherever beer-making supplies are sold. It's the heart of a beginning homebrewer's beer, a sweet, thick sauce that is boiled with water to which hops are added to make the fermentable wort. Extract can be substituted for recipes calling for molasses, corn syrup and treacle and similar thick sweeteners. It adds incredible body to a French toast mixture.

3 eggs, beaten
⅔ cup (160 mL) 10% cream
⅓ cup (80 mL) whole milk
2 tablespoons (30 mL) dark English malt extract
1 teaspoon (5 mL) vanilla
1 teaspoon (5 mL) cinnamon
Butter
10 day-old slices of bread, slightly toasted

1. Beat the eggs and mix with other ingredients, except butter and bread.

2. Melt butter in skillet or on griddle heated to medium.

3. Dip bread quickly into batter and brown in skillet on each side. Place on a platter in a warm oven until you're finished, then serve with your favourite condiments.

Blueberry Pancakes

MAKES 16 SMALL PANCAKES

I know it's an anathema for some to pop open a brew before noon, but who is it going to hurt to have a four-ounce taster glass of Folie Douce, the remarkable blueberry beer, to accompany these filling flapjacks? Or, perhaps, the maple-syrup-infused beer Tord-Vis from Le Cheval Blanc.

1½ cup (375 mL) flour
3½ teaspoons (17 mL) baking powder
½ teaspoon (2 mL) salt
⅓ cup (80 mL) sugar
1 egg, beaten
3 tablespoons (45 mL) oil
½ cup (125 mL) milk
½ cup (125 mL) Folie Douce
1 cup (250 mL) fresh or frozen blueberries
4 teaspoons (20 mL) icing sugar
Oil for frying pan or griddle

1. Mix the dry ingredients together then separately mix the wet ingredients and the fruits.

2. Stir wet mixture into dry to moisten. Don't beat.

3. Heat griddle or frying pan to medium high. Add oil to coat. Pour a ¼ cup (50 mL) of batter for each pancake onto the hot griddle or frying pan.

4. When the bottom of the pancake has browned and the batter has started to bubble, flip over to brown other side.

5. Dust with icing sugar.

Options: Use different fruit and a different, matching, or complementary, beer.

Maple Buttermilk Pancakes

MAKES 8 TO 10

In microbrewery terms, Stephen Beaumont is one of Quebec's most far-reaching exports. Beaumont was born in Westmount and lives in southern Ontario. But his Web site on the Internet, Stephen Beaumont's World of Beer (http://worldofbeer.com), is a highly informative and popular spot with all kinds of news and fun about beer, including tasting reports and recipes. Beaumont makes the rounds of beer festivals and writes about what he discovers for his Web site, several North American magazines and his own books, which include *A Taste for Beer* and *Brewpub Cookbook*.

This recipe was originally made with Niagara Falls Maple Wheat and published on the World of Beer Website, but Stephen suggests using Beauçeronne à l'Érable, the maple syrup-infused ale from Ferme Brasserie Schoune in Saint-Odilon-de-Cranbourne. Tord-Vis, the strong ale on yeast from Le Cheval Blanc, is also made with maple syrup and is suitable for this recipe.

2 cups (500 mL) flour
1½ teaspoons (7 mL) baking powder
½ teaspoon (2 mL) baking soda
2 large eggs
1 cup (250 mL) buttermilk
1 cup (250 mL) Beauceronne à l'Érable or Tord-Vis
1 teaspoon (5 mL) vanilla
2 tablespoons (30 mL) butter

1. In a large bowl, combine the flour, baking powder and baking soda. Form a well in the middle.

2. In a separate bowl, lightly beat the eggs. Add the next three ingredients and mix well. Pour the wet ingredients into the dry ingredients and mix.

3. Place a large skillet or griddle over medium heat and grease lightly with butter. Cook the pancakes until golden brown and keep in a warm oven until ready to eat. Top with butter, if desired, and real maple syrup.

Carmelized Onion and Gorgonzola Pizza

MAKES ONE 16-INCH PIZZA

Some things never change. Like my belief that pizza is the most nutritious meal around. With the right toppings, you can cover all the major food groups.

The basis of all pizza, obviously, is the dough. Get that right and the rest is pie. The carmelized onion and Gorgonzola is my current favourite but you can use any of your favourite toppings.

Pizza dough
1 tablespoon (15 mL) sugar
1 cup (250 mL) Blanche de Chambly warmed to the touch (about 110° F)
1 package dry yeast
3 cups (750 mL) all-purpose flour
1 teaspoon (5 mL) salt
½ cup (60 mL) olive oil
½ tablespoon (8 mL) cornmeal

1. Dissolve the sugar in the warmed beer. Add the yeast and stir to dissolve, about one minute. Let stand in a warm place for about five minutes, or until a thin layer of foam appears.

2. In a large bowl blend the flour and salt. Make a well in the centre and add the olive oil and yeast mixture. With a mixer, blend the ingredients (adding warm water or warm beer if the dough is too dry; or more flour if too wet). When the dough is sticky, remove to a floured board or countertop and knead until the dough is shiny, smooth and elastic—about 10 to 15 minutes.

3. Use a little olive oil to oil a bowl. Place dough in the bowl and cover with plastic wrap. Set side for 1½ hours, or until the dough has doubled in size.

4. Punch the dough down then roll out to the desired width. This quantity of dough should make one large 16-inch pizza or 2 pizzas about 10 inches in diameter, about one-quarter inch thick.

5. Preheat oven to 400° F. Lightly oil a pizza pan and evenly sprinkle it with the cornmeal. Partly bake the dough for 5-10 minutes, or until barely golden.

The topping
2 tablespoons (30 mL) Blanche de Chambly, or wheat beer
2 medium onions, cut in half then sliced crosswise
1 cup (250 mL) Gorgonzola cheese
½ cup (125 mL) grated mozzarella
2 tablespoons (30 mL) fresh thyme

1. Warm the beer in a skillet over medium-low heat. Add the onions and cook, stirring occasionally, for 30 minutes or until quite soft.

2. Crumble the Gorgonzola cheese and mix with the grated mozzarella. Sprinkle the mixture over the pizza dough. Top with the onions and thyme.

3. Return to the oven, lowered to 350°F. Bake for 10 minutes until the cheese has melted.

Trois Pistoles Rye Bread
with English Malt Glaze

MAKES 4 LOAVES

This bread is hearty with a subtle hint of lemon and a sticky-sweet glaze. A real back-to-basics recipe.

2¾ to 3¼ cups (680 mL to 810 mL) all-purpose flour
2½ cups (625 mL) rye flour
⅓ cup (80 mL) sugar
1 envelope quick-rising instant yeast
2½ teaspoons (12 mL) salt
1 tablespoon (15 mL) grated lemon peel
2 teaspoons (10 mL) caraway seeds
1 cup (250 mL) Trois Pistoles
½ cup (125 mL) water
¼ cup (60 mL) molasses
2 tablespoons (30 mL) butter
2 tablespoons (30 mL) English dark malt extract
2 tablespoons (30 mL) water

1. In a large bowl, combine 1½ cups (375 mL) of the all-purpose flour with the rye flour, sugar, dry yeast, salt, lemon rind, and caraway.

2. Heat the beer, water, molasses, and butter until very warm (about 125° F). Stir into the dry ingredients.

3. Beat 2 minutes with an electric mixer at a medium speed. Stir in enough of the remaining flour to make a soft dough. Knead 8 to 10 minutes until smooth. Cover with a towel and let rise 10 minutes.

4. Divide the dough into four equal pieces. Roll each into an oval, about 10 by 6 inches. Roll each up from the long side and taper the ends. Pinch the seams to seal. Place on a greased baking sheet. Cover again with a towel and let rise in a warm place until doubled in size (about 1½ hours.)

5. For the glaze, add the malt extract to the water and stir until well mixed. With a knife, make three diagonal cuts on top of each loaf. Brush

the loaves with the glaze. Bake at 375° F for 15 minutes, remove and brush with glaze once again. Bake an additional 10 minutes until the loaves are done.

6. Remove the loaves from the oven and place on a rack. Brush with the glaze one last time. Allow the bread to cool.

———

Soda Bread

MAKES ONE 9-INCH ROUND BREAD

S oda bread naturally combines beer and flour. Stout is the obvious choice for making this bread, which traditionally was baked over a smouldering peat fire, something the old timers say distinguished it from other breads. If you're looking for that smoky taste, perhaps a rauchbier could be substituted, or among Quebec brews, Loch Ness or McAuslan's Scotch ale. This is an adaptation of a recipe created by food writer Marcy Goldman.

1 bottle (12 oz./341 mL) stout or Scotch ale
¾ cup (180 mL) raisins
2 cups (500 mL) whole wheat flour
1 cup (250 mL) all-purpose flour
¼ cup plus 2 tablespoons (90 mL) brown sugar, packed
1 teaspoon baking soda
2½ teaspoons (12 mL) baking powder
½ teaspoon (2 mL) salt
½ teaspoon (2 mL) ground cinnamon
1 tablespoon (5 mL) caraway or fennel seeds
1 egg, beaten
¼ cup (60 mL) melted butter
1 tablespoon (15 mL) rolled oats

1. Pour the beer in a bowl and soak the raisins.

2. In a large bowl, stir together the two flours, sugar, soda, baking powder, salt, cinnamon and caraway.

3. Preheat oven to 375° F.

4. Make a well in the centre of the dry mixture and pour in the beaten egg and melted butter. Blend together. Drain the beer from the raisins and add to the batter and mix until smooth. Add the raisins.

5. Pour mixture into a greased 9-inch round cake pan. Sprinkle with the rolled oats.

6. Bake for 40 minutes. Top will crack. Remove from oven and cool on a rack before serving.

Triple Wheat Beer Biscuits

These are wonderful at anytime of day, served hot with melted butter, or with jam at breakfast.

2 cups (500 mL) all-purpose flour
1 cup (20 mL) whole wheat flour
2 tablespoons (30 mL) sugar
1½ tablespoons (22 mL) baking powder
1 teaspoon (5 mL) salt
¾ teaspoon (4 mL) cream of tartar
¾ cup (180 mL) butter
1 large egg, lightly beaten
1 bottle (12 oz./341 mL) Le Cheval Blanc's Original White Beer
2 tablespoons (30 mL) cornstarch

1. Sift two flours together and blend with sugar, baking powder, salt and cream of tartar in a large bowl. With a pastry blender, mix in butter until mixture is crumbly. Add the beaten egg and one cup (250 mL) of beer. Stir until the dough holds together.

2. Place the dough on a floured board or counter and knead until smooth. Flatten it out to a one-inch (2.54 cm) thickness. Using a floured cookie cutter, cut out biscuits and place on a lightly greased baking sheet. Put the scraps back together and continue until the dough is finished.

3. Heat oven to 425° F.

4. For the glaze, mix the beer and cornstarch in a small pot. Bring to a boil while continuously stirring. Lower the heat slightly and cook until mixture thickens. Spread glaze over the top of each biscuit.

5. Bake biscuits until browned, about 18 minutes.

Desserts

Amaretto Cookies

MAKES 3 DOZEN COOKIES

These cookies are as light as pastry, with the almonds, almond extract, and beer undercutting the sugar. We tried these while visiting friends in Vancouver. The recipe had been handed down to Baya Cavaliere from her mother, Maria. We substituted beer for the water Maria used and were incredibly happy with the results.

3 eggs
1 cup (250 mL) sugar
1 cup (250 mL) brown sugar
¾ cup (180 mL) oil
3 tablespoons (45 mL) Blanche de Chambly
1 cup (250 mL) roasted ground almonds
1 tablespoon (15 mL) baking powder
3 cups (750 mL) white flour
3 tablespoons (45 mL) pure almond extract
Confectioner's sugar, for dusting

1. Beat together the eggs, sugars, oil and beer.

2. Add the ground almonds, baking powder, flour and the almond extract. Mix then let the batter sit for one-half hour.

3. Preheat the oven to 375° F.

4. Make gumball-sized balls of batter and drop them in a bowl of the confectioner's sugar. Roll to coat. Place balls on lightly oiled cookie sheet and bake on the middle rack until cookies are golden on the bottom, about 10 minutes. Cool on rack.

Apple Blueberry Crisp

My favourite part of an apple crisp is not the apples. It's the crisp topping—darkly sweet and crunchy, just the right contrast to the tartness of the apples. The Folie Douce blueberry beer adds a tinge of bitterness to round out this dessert experience. In other versions of this recipe, I've added ¼ cup (60 mL) of another fruit, say blueberries or raspberries.

4 generous cups (1 L) sliced Granny Smith apples
1 teaspoon (5 mL) cinnamon
¼ cup (60 mL) Folie Douce
1 cup (250 mL) flour
½ cup (125 mL) white sugar
½ cup (125 mL) dark brown sugar
½ cup (125 mL) softened butter

1. Grease 10x6x2-inch baking dish. Place apples evenly in dish. Sprinkle with cinnamon and pour beer over.

2. Mix remaining ingredients together until relatively smooth. Pour entire mixture over fruit.

3. Bake at 350° F for about 40 minutes, or until flour and sugar mixture on top is a deep golden brown.

Cheddar and Ale Cheesecake

The night President Kennedy was shot, my wife, Denise was a sixteen-year-old seated at the dinner table with her parents, enthralled by author John A. Williams. He was in Los Angeles working on a new book, a black man's travelogue across the United States called *This is My Country Too*.

As told by Denise's mom, Jackie Roig, the death of Kennedy was never mentioned, though Denise remembers laughter that offered little comfort. In John's book, he describes Jackie's cheesecake made with beer.

This is a variation of that original recipe—a memory of the early 1960s, a reminder of those events that are forever behind us. The crust includes a fruit preserve. Since there are so many Quebec fruit beers on the market (from apricot to blueberry and cherry), why not choose your dessert beer to match or contrast the preserve in the cake?

1½ cups (375 mL) vanilla wafer or graham cracker crumbs
½ cup (125 mL) melted unsalted butter
⅓ cup (80 mL) fruit preserve (we had raspberry on hand)
2 pounds (1 kg) cream cheese
½ cup (125 mL) freshly grated mild yellow cheddar cheese
1½ cups (375 mL) sugar
1 teaspoon (5 mL) vanilla
4 eggs
2 egg yolks
¼ cup (60 mL) 35% cream
¼ cup (60 mL) Maudite

1. Preheat oven to 300° F.

2. Mix the wafer crumbs and butter together, then press into the bottom and around sides of a 9-inch springform pan. Spread the preserve over the crust.

3. Beat the cream cheese until soft, then add the chedda,r beating continuously. Gradually stir in the sugar and vanilla. Beat in the eggs and yolks, one at a time. Continue beating until smooth.

4. Fold in the cream and beer. Pour filling into crust.

5. Bake for 1½ hours. Turn off oven, and with oven door ajar, keep the cake inside for another 30 minutes. Cool on a rack. Chill before serving.

Double the Chocolate Double the Fun Cake

MAKES ONE 9-INCH CAKE

This is a densely chocolate cake, made without flour, with just a touch of stout and malt extract for added body.

Cake
12 ounces (375 mL) bittersweet chocolate, chopped
¾ cup (180 mL) unsalted butter, cut in pieces
6 large eggs, separated
¾ cup (180 mL) sugar
1 tablespoon (15 mL) Boréale Noire

1. Preheat oven to 350° F. Line the bottom of a nine-inch springform pan with waxed paper, butter the paper and sides of pan. Wrap the outside of the pan with foil.

2. Stir chocolate and butter, one piece at a time, in a saucepan over low heat until melted smooth. Remove from heat and cool to lukewarm, stirring often.

3. In a large bowl, beat the egg yolks and 6 tablespoons (90 mL) of sugar with a mixer until the mixture is thick, about three minutes. Fold the lukewarm chocolate into the egg yolk mixture, then fold in the stout.

4. In a separate bowl, beat the egg whites until soft peaks form. Gradually add the remaining sugar, beating until medium firm peaks form. Fold the egg whites into the chocolate mixture by thirds. Pour the entire batter into the pan.

5. Bake the cake until the top puffs, is cracked, and a tester comes out of the centre with some moist crumbs attached, about 45 to 50 minutes. Cool the cake on a rack. Don't worry when the cake falls.

6. Gently press down on the top to even it out. With a knife, loosen the cake from the sides of the pan. Remove the pan sides and place a tart pan bottom or round cardboard on top of the cake. Invert the cake onto the bottom and peel off the waxed paper.

Glaze
½ cup (125 mL) 35% whipping cream
¼ cup (60 mL) corn syrup
¼ cup (60 mL) dark malt extract
9 ounces (270 mL) bittersweet chocolate, chopped

1. Bring the cream, corn syrup, and extract to simmer in a saucepan. Remove from heat and add the chocolate. Whisk until chocolate is melted and mixture is smooth.

2. Place the cake on its rack on a baking sheet. Spread half the glaze over the cake's top and sides. Place in freezer until almost set—about three minutes. Pour the remaining glaze over the cake. Smooth all around. Place the cake on a platter and chill it until the glaze is firm. Serve at room temperature.

Option: Substitute the corn syrup by doubling the amount of malt extract, which is available at any beermaking supply shop.

Chocolate Stout Mousse

One flavour combination many people have a hard time getting their minds around is beer and chocolate. Beer is just too bitter; the chocolate just too sweet. But porter and stout often have chocolate notes in the nose and the palate. My wife, Denise, made this with La Pacômois, a fermented raspberry drink made in Saint-Pacôme, Quebec, but it could just as easily, and just as tastily, be made with kirsch, the cherry liqueur, Grand Marnier, Amaretto, Kahlua, or other distilled or fermented fruit beverages. It is based on a recipe by author and restaurateur Candy Schermerhorn.

9 ounces (270 mL) bittersweet chocolate
6 tablespoons (90 mL) St. Ambroise Oatmeal Stout
2 tablespoons (30 mL) fruit liqueur, such as kirsch, Grand Marnier,
or Amaretto
4 eggs at room temperature before separating
1 cup (250 mL) 35% cream
½ teaspoon (2 mL) vanilla
¼ cup (60 mL) sugar
¼ teaspoon (1 mL) cream of tartar

1. Melt the chocolate in a double boiler, stirring constantly, then add stout and liqueur. Mix well. Remove from heat.

2. Add one yolk at a time to the chocolate mixture, beating after each addition. Then set aside.

3. In a separate bowl, whip the cream, vanilla and sugar together until stiff peaks form. Refrigerate.

4. In a clean mixing bowl, with clean beaters, beat the egg whites and cream of tartar until stiff. Fold the beaten whites with the whipped cream. Fold half of mixture into the chocolate and mix until no white shows. Incorporate the balance and mix until no white shows. Serve in wine goblets or mousse dishes with a thin mint cookie.

Griffon Coffee Cake

Ten percent yogurt and the fullness of Griffon Blonde are the secrets to the mouth feel of this coffee cake. Yogurt with less fat just doesn't cut it.

¾ cup (180 mL) softened butter
1½ cups (375 mL) sugar
3 eggs
1½ teaspoons (8 mL) vanilla
1½ cups (375 mL) 10% yogurt or sour cream
3 cups (750 mL) flour
1½ teaspoons (8 mL) baking soda
1½ teaspoons (8 ml) baking powder
½ cup (125 mL) Griffon Blonde
½ cup (125 mL) brown sugar
⅔ cup (160 mL) chopped pecans
2 teaspoons (10 mL) cinnamon

1. Preheat oven to 350° F.

2. Cream the butter in a large mixing bowl, adding the sugar gradually until the mixture is light and fluffy.

3. Beat in the eggs one at a time, mixing well after each is added.

4. Stir in the vanilla and yogurt.

5. Sift the flour, baking soda, and baking powder together.

6. Add beer to the egg mixture, alternating with the sifted dry ingredients. Beat the batter until it is well blended.

7. Mix brown sugar, chopped pecans, and cinnamon. Place one-third of the nut mixture at the bottom of a well-greased tube or angel-food cake pan.

8. Layer in one-third of the batter, and continue, alternating between the nut mixture and batter.

9. Bake in the oven for one hour. Cool on rack.

Granité à la Folie Douce

This blueberry-beer ice, from Christian Lévêque of Montreal's Inter-Continental Hotel, reminds me of the Italian ices we used to have as kids.

4/5 cup (200 mL) water
1 cup (250 mL) sugar
1 bottle (12 oz./341 mL) Folie Douce

1. Bring water and sugar to a boil, simmer and cook until syrupy, then chill.

2. Add the beer to 1 cup (250 mL) of the syrup in a shallow metal bowl. Freeze.

3. Scrape the frozen mixture with a fork, mix, then refreeze. Repeat once or twice until desired consistency is reached.

———

Oven-Baked Berries Macerated in Blueberry Beer

SERVES 5

Two hearts beat as one. There are two essentials to this fine dessert, the sabayon (or zabaglione) and the berries. Bringing them together is a match made in culinary heaven, or at least in Christian Lévêque's kitchen.

1 cup (250 mL) 35% cream
5 egg yolks
4/5 cup (200 mL) sugar
4 tablespoons (60 mL) water
Berries (blackberry, raspberry, blueberry, strawberry, in any combination desired)
⅔ cup (160 mL) Folie Douce

Sabayon

1. Whip the cream until it forms stiff peaks. Set aside.

2. Beat the eggs until foamy.

3. Mix together the sugar and water and heat to 120°F. Slowly pour this mixture into the beaten eggs and mix until completely incorporated and not grainy. Fold whipped cream into egg mixture and refrigerate.

The berries

1. Place a handful of berries in five oven-proof bowls along with 2 tablespoons (30 mL) of beer. Heat in 400° F for 5 minutes. Divide the sabayon evenly among the bowls and return them to the oven until the sabayon turns golden. Serve immediately.

———

Poached Pears in Traditional Amber Beer

SERVES 4

This is the perfect dessert when you think you ate too much and couldn't eat another thing! Another from Chef Christian Lévêque.

4 pears
1 bottle (12 oz./341 mL) Cheval Blanc Traditional Amber Beer
1 cup (250 mL) sugar
2 3-inch (7.5 cm) cinnamon sticks
Vanilla ice cream

1. Peel the pears and place in a pot with the beer, sugar and cinnamon sticks. Simmer over a medium-to-low heat for about 20 minutes. Remove pears and refrigerate. Continue cooking the liquid until reduced by half.

2. Before serving, thinly slice the pears and arrange in a circle around each plate. Place a scoop of vanilla ice cream in the centre and pour the syrup over the ice cream and the pears.

Cherry Zabaglione

At some point in culinary history the Italian zabaglione became universally known as sabayon. Zabaglione was traditionally made with Marsala wine; Chef Christian Lévêque uses Unibroue's Quelque Chose cherry beer for a unique new twist on an old favourite.

6 egg yolks
⅔ cup (160 mL) sugar
¾ cup (180 mL) Quelque Chose
1¼ cup (310 mL) 35% heavy cream

1. With an electric mixer, blend together the yolks and sugar. Add beer and mix until smooth.

2. Warm the yolk mixture in a double-boiler to 112° F. (Have your candy thermometer ready because it won't take long to reach the required heat. You want to avoid cooking the yolks.) Remove from heat and beat until the mixture is smooth and thick.

3. Whip cream in a separate bowl until it is stiff and airy. Gently fold the whipped cream into the yolk mixture.

4. Pour into wine glasses or dessert bowls, and refrigerate—or freeze for a Cherry Zabaglione Ice Cream.

Unibroue's Maudite, like Dow Old Stock Ale, evokes the Quebec
folk tale of loggers who have sold their souls to Satan.

Cheese and Beer

Cheese and Beer: How Natural

High school friends still tease me about the night I showed up at a restaurant with my new girlfriend. They, and their dates, were comfortably ensconced on sofas and overstuffed chairs in the bar area drinking beer and munching on nuts. When the waitress asked what we wanted, my girlfriend ordered for the both of us: white Zinfandel and a cheese platter.

It was a mistake. My friends choked on their honey-roasteds. The girlfriend? Well, it didn't last.

Wine has dictated our cultural palates forever, it seems. Beer, since its arrival in Canada 350 years ago, has been treated as less than equal, the drink of the great unwashed. Well, count me in among them. I know who my friends are.

Partly this elitism toward wine can be traced to the French influence in North American, especially Québécois, cuisines. In the United States, that happened in the 1940s after the Second World War; in Quebec and Canada, France has always been a factor. Wine is part of the history and culture we read in books, live on the streets, and eat in restaurants. A spread of cheese, for example, laid out after a baptism or at any celebration will include baguette slices and wine.

There's a wine for every cheese, the saying goes, and since the micro-brewery revolution began twenty years ago in Massachusetts, one can say just as proudly and loudly: There is also a beer for every cheese. So slide that bottle of vino aside and pull out a six.

We find ourselves at the beginning of a new century holding beer and cheese parties. It's the hip new thing. That this most blessed of marriages still hasn't caught on with the œnophiles and elitists—and might never—is OK. I'll just pull up a chair here with my fellow beer-drinkers Gilles Jourdenais, co-owner of the Fromagerie du Marché Atwater, and Mario D'Eer, author of several Quebec beer guides, and former director of the Festibière once held in Chambly, Quebec.

Jourdenais has arranged tastings for Quebec microbreweries, and even the Fourquet Fourchette restaurant in Chambly, whose entire menu is given over to dishes prepared with and accompanied by Unibroue products.

One of the fascinations for Jourdenais is the experimentation. "Cheeses change from region to region and season to season. I have right now five different Gruyère from Switzerland, all with different flavours and their own characteristics," he said. Each one of those cheeses could demand a different beer.

"I prefer the combination of hard cheeses with beer, I find they go much nicer together," Jourdenais said. "It's more difficult to pair soft cheese with beer, but that's just my opinion. Some soft cheeses go better with wine. Harder cheeses are aged longer, so the salt crystals give it a tangier flavour. You can have a variety of sweet or pungent or more sour or more salty."

Jourdenais considers Ossau-Iraty, a sheep's milk cheese from the Pyrenées, a fantastic match for a sharp ale like Maudite from Unibroue. But his favourite is Victor et Berthold, a semi-soft ripened 100-percent raw cow's milk cheese made in Notre-Dame-de-Lourdes, near Joliette, Quebec. He pairs it with St. Ambroise Pale Ale, although he also recommends Blonde McChouffe, brewed in Quebec by Le Cheval Blanc, a combination he was reluctant to try at first but which won him over.

Mario D'Eer has had lots of requests to hold tastings of beer and cheese, for business meetings for example, where people don't know anything about wine and cheese or beer and cheese, but just recognize the tasting as something fashionable. He has a theory about wine and cheese vs. beer and cheese that sounds like my theory about girlfriends and old high-school chums. "Wine and cheese don't really mix," D'Eer said.

But before you wine-lovers get your grapes in a bunch, allow him his say: "Instead, the tastes run parallel in your mouth. It will always be good. Beer, on the other hand, mixes with cheese, so when it's bad, you know it's bad."

So there's the challenge: to find the right beer to go with the right cheese. "I compare it to human relationships—a love affair when it turns sour, it turns sour," D'Eer added. "Beer and cheese is not better than wine and cheese, but it is different."

Stephen Beaumont, author of several Canadian beer guides including *A Taste for Beer*, says beer and cheese go so well together because they are essentially both products of aging processes. D'Eer, too, thinks there is an elementally similar nature: "Think of beer as liquid bread, you'll find that the grain or cereal that is the structure of beer is similar to that in bread, and nothing goes better with cheese than bread. In many beers, those grains are roasted, so think of roasted crackers. That's why St. Ambroise Oatmeal Stout goes with absolutely any cheese. When you play with sweetness and roasted taste of beer, you can have 10,000 matches."

But D'Eer cautions: "It's the beer's bitterness where you have to be very careful, the bitterness of the hops. Blue cheese and hops, for example, don't go together. But with a young brie and young Camembert, the bitterness gets to the cream from the cheese and it turns smooth in the mouth."

A few points before serving

When you are buying your cheese, smell it first. Any cheese that smells "off"—an ammonia-like scent is a good indicator something ain't right—avoid it. Bring the cheese out to room temperature for an hour before serving. Cover with a damp cloth to conserve the cheese's natural humidity, and if you serve a number of cheeses on the same platter, be careful not to have them touch, which could mix flavors. Use a separate knife or cheese cutter for each cheese for the same reason.

Pairing cheese and beer

When choosing a beer to accompany a cheese, you may consider the advice of Beaumont: "Strong with strong and mild with mild." With this model in mind, have GMT's Belle Gueule with a bagel and cream cheese; Stilton or Danish blue cheese with Boréale Noire; Eau Bénite with Brick cheese; Raftman with Gruyère.

Or you might consider Jourdenais' advice that taste is entirely personal. "My favorite, the Victor et Berthold, is already a classic though it's been only six years. I gave some to my neighbor, he doesn't like it. But he likes Guinness and so do I. But he thinks it's sharp and has it with different cheese than I do.

"There are some guidelines and if you stay within guidelines, you'll find your own personal favorite," he said. There are as many cheese available in Quebec as there are beers, so finding exactly the right match is a matter of trial-and-error.

Some suggestions

Lagers and light pale ales or wheat ales, like Unibroue's U and Blanche de Chambly, Belle Gueule or Griffon and Boréale Blonde, are best accompanied by havarti, or a soft cow's milk cheese with a downy rind, like a mild brie.

Alongside a red or amber beer, like Boréale Rousse, St. Ambroise Pale Ale, serve Oka or Sir Laurier d'Arthabaska, Saint-Damase (pressed cow's milk cheeses with washed rinds), a blue-veined goat cheese like Bleu de Castello, Camembert or a mild Gouda.

Marry Griffon Brown or Maudite with a strong cheddar. Maudite is also recommended with Barbu, Mamirolle and Fêtard.

Danesbourg herb cheese or Oka Classic, a stronger version of the regular Oka, are natural accompaniments to strong ales. Among Quebec craft beers, these include Boréale Cuivrée and Trois Pistoles.

Serve McAuslan's Scotch Ale with a smoked Gouda or Danesbourg or smoked Gruyère.

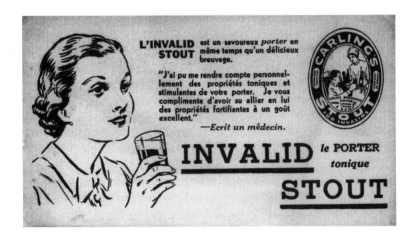

Dow Brewery's origins are in Montreal, where it was founded
by Scotsman William Dow.

Drinks

Mixed Drinks

There was beer long before distilled liquors and wine. Mixed drinks or cocktails were served by Colonial Americans and Canadians, and by Englishmen for years before them. They used beers as the base for their drinks, infusing them with herbs and spices, and adding fruit, milk or eggs. Distilled liquors were eventually added to the beer, too. The wassail bowl we sing about at Christmas time is such a drink, comprising half a dozen spices, a gallon of beer, almost a litre of sherry, sugar, a dozen apples and a dozen eggs. Often the best cocktails are nothing more simple than mixing two types of beer styles together. Here are some favourites.

Blonde on Blonde

Like the Bob Dylan album, this can go to your head. There are any number of variations, but the idea is to mix a white (wheat) with a blonde (lager). Whites include Blanche de Chambly, Cheval Blanc's Original White Beer. Blondes include Boréale Blonde, Griffon Blonde, Belle Gueule, Illegal, U. The list and permutations are not endless, but almost.

Black and Tan

Also known as a Half and Half, or an 'arf and 'arf. Mix equal parts of stout with a pale ale.

Cherry Stout

Pour together equal parts of St. Ambroise Oatmeal Stout and Quelque Chose.

Black Velvet

Usually this is made with stout and champagne, but try mixing a stout with an equal amount of Mystique, the apple cider bottled by McAuslan Brewery.

Shandy

Equal parts chilled ginger beer, or ginger ale, and lager.

Øl Grog

Øl is the Norwegian for ale, or beer. This is a winter warmer made by simmering a bottle of lager, like Belle Gueule (which, incidentally, is French for "big mouth"), together with one tablespoon (15 mL) of white rum and one teaspoon (5 mL) of powdered sugar.

White Water

Simply, this is a Depth-Charged Boilermaker using Raftman beer from Unibroue. Raftman is made with whisky malt and the White Water is made by dropping a shot glass of whisky straight into a pint glass of Raftman.

The Flip

This was popular in the early 1700s and the name comes from the flip-flopping of beer from one pitcher to another. An ordinary ale would have been used and a red-hot poker would be inserted into the concoction to give it a toasty taste. Instead, I would suggest 1837, which is just hearty enough as a base. Pour two bottles of 1837 and ½-cup (125 mL) of gin into a sauce pan and heat through, but not to a boil. Remove from heat and add two beaten eggs and two tablespoons (30 mL) of sugar. Pour back and forth between two pitchers until frothy and serve in a large tankard.

Red-Eye

This is from the Canadian West. Fill half a glass with a lager and the rest with tomato juice.

Prairie Oyster

Another Western concoction. Fill a glass with a lager and crack a raw egg into it. The white will disappear and the yoke will sink to the bottom like a ball. Sip the beer slowly, swallowing the slightly pickled egg at the end.

Cocktail Bonnefemme

The Brewers Association of Canada recommends boiling two bottles of beer (I would suggest a wheat beer), with a pinch of ginger and cinnamon bark for three minutes. Pour in 2 tablespoons (30 mL) of fresh lemon juice and boil for another minute. Pass through a sieve, refrigerate for two hours, then serve on ice.

Quelle Frappé

For an experience that is truly something else, use Quelque Chose, Unibroue's cherry beer. You wouldn't think that this works. But man!

1 bottle (12 oz./340 mL) Quelque Chose
Two scoops vanilla ice cream
¼ teaspoon (1 mL) balsamic vinegar
½ teaspoon (2 mL) vanilla

Blend all ingredients in a blender, then serve in a tall glass.

Panaché à la Blanche

SERVES 2

Juice of 2 large lemons
1 cup (250 mL) Blanche de Chambly
½ cup (125 mL) sugar
Cold water
Ice cubes

1. In a quart jug mix the lemon juice, beer, sugar and water. Fill with ice cubes and serve immediately.

Variation
Use the juice of two oranges and a lime with a bottle of the Cheval Blanc's Original White Beer for an orangeade with punch.

A History, Comprehensive and Containing
Certain Facts and Subjectivities,
of Beer and Brewing in the
Province of Quebec,
from the Landing of Cartier
to the Advent of
Microbreweries

Playing cards were given by breweries as sales incentives to their best customers. Decks of Champlain India Pale Ale cards were distributed in the 1920s.

The First Beer in Canada

The Vikings first set foot on Newfoundland about one thousand years ago. Leif Ericsson actually named the place Vinland, but surely not for the grape. These Norse sea-kings were inveterate imbibers, who never left their native Iceland without ale, which they called "aul," onboard. The Vikings would have been the first Europeans to drink beer in North America, almost six hundred years before the "lost colony" in Virginia or before the *Mayflower* struck rock because its captain got thirsty. The Vikings left in 1347 before they could make a lasting impression on either the history or culture of North America, never mind our beer drinking. So we jump ahead half a millennium.

The crowds gathered at the quay as the noble voyagers prepare to embark. "Where are you off to, sir?" "The Indies, perhaps China," the sailor replied. "Don't drink the water!" Water, the French knew, caused illness aboard ship and could become putrid and undrinkable. Beer, whose alcohol kills off pesky bacteria, has more staying power. But the British, French, and other Europeans, three and four hundred years ago, didn't know bacteria from backgammon. Because some of the water of their own creeks, brooks, rivers, and lakes had become polluted and disease-ridden, they assumed all water was that way, not realizing that it was the boiling of water during the brewing process that did away with most impurities in their beer.

The history of beer in Canada reads, essentially, like the history of the nation itself. And the history of beer in Canada begins with a concoction most North Americans today have never tried—spruce beer. The early explorers ascribed medicinal properties to it, and with good reason. On one of Jacques Cartier's later voyages, some members of the crew got scurvy. They were restored to health and their lives were saved because they drank spruce beer. Cartier's first trip, with ale aboard, was in 1534, fifty years before a colony was established in Virginia, and seventy years before a Captain George Weymouth grew barley in the northern part of that state. Cartier borrowed the idea of spicing his crew's beer with spruce after encounters with native Indians, who used spruce as an infusion. More than likely, Indians would not have brewed beer. The ingredients weren't here, just as they weren't in Roanoke, Virginia, when the English landed in 1584. Thomas Hariot, who wrote of that first attempted foothold in North America, found "barlie, oates and peaze" growing naturally, but no evidence of hops.

The distinction of first beer-makers in North America goes to Adrian Block and Hans Christiansen, who opened a brewery in New Amsterdam on Manhattan island in 1612, with imported ingredients.

The French who explored and settled the uncharted territory of northern America in the late 1500s and early 1600s were from regions known for their cider- and beer-making. Samuel de Champlain began a French colony in Canada in 1603. In Paris in 1612, Champlain recruited four Recollet missionaries to minister in New France. The Recollet fathers began brewing in Quebec in 1620 (the year the Pilgrims landed at Plimouth Rock).

Louis Hébert, a Parisian apothecary and herbalist with an adventurous soul, arrived in New France in 1604 with Pierre de Gast, Sieur des Monts, and worked at Port-Royal for several years. There he befriended Champlain, who invited him to Quebec, to L'Habitation. Hébert did, thus becoming Quebec's first settler. Hébert is recorded in 1627 as having a cauldron that was used to make beer for the family, although in all likelihood it was his wife, Marie Rollet, who did the brewing. She aided her husband in his profession and helped educate Indian children. The Recollet priests persuaded Rollet to put up a special batch of beer at a feast in Notre-Dame-des-Anges, for the baptism of Naneogauchit, son of the Montagnais chief Chomina, at which they hoped to attract more souls for Christianity.

When Hébert died, he willed the cauldron to the community. His sons and daughters are numerous among those of French-Canadian ancestry today and I am honoured that I can trace my paternal line to fellow homebrewers Louis Hébert and his wife, Marie Rollet.

A story is related that Champlain, who became Quebec's first governor, used a brewing cauldron, most likely the Héberts', to prepare the Huron stew sagamité for a feast with the Indians in August 1633. (Now, of course, even homebrewers are cautious not to let their brew kettles be "contaminated" with other foodstuffs.)

The Recollets' stay in Quebec was short, but their legacy is one Canadians share each time they pop open a cool one, though I doubt the good friars had musical twist-off caps on their minds when missionary Denis Jamet wrote, from their establishment on the St. Charles River: "We hope that in two years we will be able to sustain twelve persons without anything asked from France, because we will have sufficient grain to make bread and beer." In 1629 the order was forced to leave by the English, but they returned in 1670 to establish a parish at Trois-Rivières. Louis Hébert's widow, Marie Rollet, and her daughter Guillemette's family lived among the Montagnais until 1632 when the French returned.

One of the greatest sources of information about Canada's early history is *The Jesuit Relations*, a series of long letters written by the members of the Society of Jesus in New France to the home office in France. In his letter summarizing the events of 1634, Paul LeJeune, the Jesuits' first Superior in Canada, confirmed the necessity "to procure for the community the drink for which it has need. ... We shall have to make some beer; but we shall wait until ... a brewery is erected." And in time, it was so, but not at the hands of the Society of Jesus. A brewery co-operative was begun by the settlers of Quebec in 1634. In a 1636 letter the Jesuit Superior details the diet of a farm labourer in the new colony: an allowance of flour, lard, oil and vinegar, cod, and peas. Plus, "they are given a chopine [a pint] of cider a day, or a quart of beer, and occasionally a drink of wine, as on feast days. In the winter they are given a drop of brandy in the morning." Eleven years later the Jesuits built a rather primitive brewery at Sillery. Brother Ambroise Cauvet was the brewmaster, with a mandate to make "cru and beer."

That the religious orders were brewers was in keeping with the tradition of Europe, where for hundreds of years the monks made ale, and other beverages. Beer was seen as a healthy drink, compared to water and to distilled spirits that caused drunken and lascivious behaviour. Opening a brewery was also one way priests could control settlers' lifestyles.

In 1666, Jean Talon, the intendant in charge of economic development and the legal system in New France, submitted a business plan for a brewery to his supervisor Jean Colbert, chief minister to Louis XIV. "If the use of beer is introduced for good in Canada and the people get accustomed to it, as they should, for the beverage is good and healthy in itself and a good deal less expensive than wine or alcohol, the money will remain in the country and drunkenness and the vices which generally accompany it shall no longer be the cause of scandal, by reason of the cold nature of beer, the vapors whereof rarely deprive men of the use of judgment."

The clincher was his appeal regarding the purse strings of Mother France: "Beer could also profitably enter the trade. I can guarantee two thousand barrels a year for the islands and more if the consumption is greater, without altering the supply to the colonists of New France. It is by these methods that His Majesty will succeed in his aim of destroying the trade of the Dutch in our islands, without depriving his subjects residing there of the support they derived from it."

Colbert approved the plan and the Brasserie du Roi was commissioned.

François LeMercier, the Jesuit Provincial, wrote to his superior, Étienne des Champs:

A brewery which M. Talon is having built will also contribute not only to the public welfare by forcing a decrease in the use of intoxicating drinks, which occasions a great lawlessness here; that can be obviated by using this other drink, which is very wholesome and not injurious. Moreover it will keep in the country the money which is now being sent out of it in purchase of so much liquor in France. It will also promote consumption of the super-abundance of grain which has sometimes been so great that the laborers can not find a market for it.

The equipment for Talon's brewery came from France and included two large kettles. The building was erected at the foot of Ste. Geneviève's Hill in Quebec City, a short distance from the shipbuilding yards on the St. Charles River. It was not, however, a hit, even though a royal decree signed March 5, 1668, tried to help by limiting the colony to eight hundred barrels of wine and four hundred of whiskey a year. The Brasserie du Roi produced four thousand hogsheads (barrels) of beer, half of which was intended for export to the West Indies, at a wholesale cost of $4 per hogshead. (A hogshead is the equivalent of 432 pints of beer.) The brewery failed, however, because wine and hard liquors continued to be imported, often by smuggling. Cost was also a factor. Even the governor, de Frontenac, thought the beer was too expensive. The West Indian exportation scheme was a bust, and in 1675 the brewery closed. Talon offered the building to the king for use as a general hospital, but that was refused. Eventually the building was sold to Intendant de Meulles for 30,000 livres. It was known as the Palais de l'Intendant until fire destroyed it in 1713.

Other Early Breweries

In 1670 another commercial craft brewery joined Talon's in Quebec—the Brasserie de l'Habitation. Farther up the St. Lawrence River, the Brasserie de Montréal set up shop. We know the brewery existed before October 22, 1650, because a marriage contract between Louis Prud'homme and Roberte Gadois contained a dated deed declaring a gift of thirty arpents (acres) to the newlyweds. The gift, from Paul de Chomedey, Sieur de Maisonneuve, one of the city's founders, was land near the Fort of Ville-Marie, "contiguous to the property of the Brewery, on one side and that of Michel Chauvin, dit Sainte-Suzanne, on the other."

On May 10, 1651, about two o'clock in the morning, about forty Iroquois tried to set fire to the Brasserie de Montréal. The four French guards who were sleeping nearby woke up and repelled them.

A brewery was established across the St. Lawrence River from Montreal in 1670; twenty years later, Charles le Moyne, Seigneur de Longueuil, had erected a masonry brewhouse near the fort there. The building still existed in 1735, though in ruins, when the grounds were sold to François Lanctôt to build a home.

By the early eighteenth century, Montreal, Canada's largest city, had six breweries, their clientele mostly labourers and colonists. Quebec was run on a seigneurial system; in Montreal the seigneurs were the Sulpicians, who ran their religious institutions, and therefore the city, with an iron fist. The Charron order of brothers came to know that fist in 1704 when they built a brewery at Point St. Charles for the poor people who were entrusted to their care. Grain for the breweries came from one miller, but the Charron brothers found the existing supply insufficient for their needs and built their own mill. The Sulpicians insisted on their monopoly and refused to administer the sacraments to the brothers until the mill was demolished. The compromise, in the end, was that the Charron brothers were allowed to keep their mill if they milled only what they needed for the brewery and the soldiers garrisoned in Montreal. However, the soldiers rarely paid their bills and the debt forced the Charrons to lease their brewery to Pierre Braban and Pierre Crépeau in December 1708.

For several decades, a handful of small breweries supplied kegs of ale to local public houses, trying to establish a bit of brand loyalty, if we can attach such a twentieth-century concept to an eighteenth-century practice. Breweries would fail; others would start up.

Early Drinking Habits

Beer consumption remained lower than the consumption of wines, brandies, and other spirits imported from Europe. The list of liquors available to the early settlers of New France hardly differs from what one finds now in Quebec. The settlers had access to brandy, rum, Spanish and French wines, sherry-like madeira, the sweet muscat-grape malaga, and anisette. Beer-drinking colonists drank, like all beer-drinkers, a cloudy, basically flat, hopped ale of about six percent alcohol. Lagering had yet to be invented, and often barley and hops had to be imported. Wheat or corn was sometimes used instead of barley, and instead of hops, spruce. Spruce could even replace the grain.

One type of beer made during this time was called "bouillon." The early settlers who had come from Picardy and Upper Normandy in France brought this recipe with them. A ball of raw dough made from wheat or maize was allowed to ferment in a vat of spiced water, then that fermented wort was further diluted with water and allowed to age in wooden casks. It was a poor man's beer, but better than water since it had a kick to it. It was sold as late as 1670 and was sometimes used as barter with Indians for pelts.

While on a return visit to France in 1663, the governor of Trois-Rivières, Pierre Boucher, said of his fellow Canadians: "Usually, wine is served only in wealthy families, beer among the less fortunate, and a drink called 'bouillon' in practically all other families."

The Swedish botanist Peter Kalm mentioned spruce beer in his description of the Quebec table, which included bread of wheat flour, soups,

> every kind of fresh meat, boiled and roasted, by game, fowls, fricasséed or stewed in casseroles, all served with various sorts of salad. ... After dinner there is dessert, which comprises a variety of fruit, walnuts from France or Canada, either fresh or preserved, almonds, grapes, hazelnuts, various species of berry which ripen in the summer, such as currants and cranberries crystallized in molasses, sweet jams made of strawberries, raspberries, blackberries, and other briar fruits. Cheese also appears with the dessert, as well as milk which is taken at the end of the meal with sugar.

Kalm wrote that the well-to-do would not drink beer, especially the summer-available spruce variety. "People of quality," he said in 1749, spent their money on imported wine.

The Effects of War

In 1759 the long-standing conflict between France and England over their North American colonies exploded into the Battle of the Plains of Abraham at Quebec City. New France was formally ceded in 1763. During this period soldiers on both sides of the war drank a beer-like concoction of spruce, pine, molasses, and raw sugar. British General James Wolfe, who was to die on the Plains of Abraham, had, like the French adventurer Cartier before him, ascribed anti-scorbutic properties to spruce beer and insisted his troops drink it to avoid incapacitation by scurvy. Spruce beer was also a hit with Benjamin Franklin, who took a shining to it on a trip to France, where he was envoy from the United States. A recipe for spruce beer was set forth in an inexact

exact kind of way, by British General Jeffrey Amherst:

> Take seven pounds of good Spruce & boil it well till the bark peels off, then take the Spruce out & put three Gallons of Molasses to the Liquor & boil it again, scum it well as it boils, then take it out the kettle & put it into a cooler, boil the remained of the water sufficient for a Barrel of thirty Gallons, if the kettle is not large enough to boil it together, when milk-warm in the Cooler put a Pint of Yest into it and mix well. Then put in the Barrel and let it work for two or three days, keep filling it up as it works out. When done working, bung it up with a Tent Peg in the Barrel to give it vent every now and then. It may be used in two or three days after. If wanted to be bottled it should stand a fortnight in the Cask. It will keep a great while.

The war had a devastating effect on brewing. At the time Canada became British property there were no breweries in Quebec and the revenue derived from wine importation evaporated. Wrote Governor Sir James Murray: "Those, who were in the habit of drinking it, had returned to France."

The American Revolution had a positive effect on the state of brewing in Quebec. Taverns and breweries were so important to the economic well-being of the colonies and the physical well-being of the colonists—it was better to drink beer than water—that the taxes levied upon the Americans for goods like imported liquor or the special permits needed to serve beer, were considered intolerable, and led, not as indirectly as one might think, to the war for independence. One of the Continental Congress' first acts, in 1755, was to order a ration of one pint a day per soldier.

Not all the colonists believed in the war and many followed the Hudson River and Lake Champlain north into Quebec. These were the United Empire Loyalists and their legacy, at least as far as beer is concerned, is the restoration of the brewing industry in Quebec and the prevailing preference of Quebecers to ale over lager.

Founding the Molson Brewery

When John Molson arrived in Montreal from England in the early 1780s, Quebecers preferred their French-imported wine and spirits. But there was a market for beer in Montreal where there were many British immigrants, as well as Loyalists from the United States, and British troops. Molson, though he was underage—not the last time beer and underage found themselves in the same sentence—was interested in forming a partnership with Thomas Loid (also spelled Loyd), who was "erecting a malting house new from the ground and there is no fear of it answering if he brings it to perfection as he proposes to sell beer at £5 per hogshead." It was a little log brewhouse at the foot of the St. Lawrence River rapids called St. Mary's Current, near St. Helen's Island. Loid's brewery came into "perfection" that first year, 1783. Molson became a full partner of Loid and they hired a full-time brewmaster, John Wait. In 1785, Molson bought out his partner for sole control of the brewery.

In a letter to relatives in England, dated December 13, 1786, Molson wrote: "The speculation now is beginning to show in good Ale and Table Beer—I can acquaint my Friend that my beer has the readiest sale and orders are by one half more than can execute." Two years later, sales quadrupled to 258 hogsheads.

The beer John Molson brewed in 1786 would be unfamiliar to most North Americans now. It was all malt, giving it a full body and mouth feel, with no additives or adjuncts like rice or corn. "Some were heavily hopped, some less, but keep in mind those were the days that beers tended to have a lot of bitterness to them. This made them quite distinct," said Ian Stanners, director of brewing for Molson, in an interview. Stanners reached behind where he was sitting in his office and removed a handwritten logbook from his bookshelf. He opened the log to April 1, 1908:

> They made an India pale ale on that day. Look, the brewer's put down the temperature of the air outside, and the water temperature. He's got a nice selection of hops, Oregon, New Canadian. It's the normal fermentation temperature for ale, about twenty degrees (Celsius) and, true to an IPA, they threw into the fermenter fifty pounds of English hops. This would have given it a really hoppy nose.

He pointed out first that what would almost be considered hop overload by today's standards was done for health reasons: hops had an antiseptic quality and on voyages to India the hops guarded against infection.

Even early Molson standards like its Stock Ale and Export, brewed to this day, were originally more heavily hopped. "This added to the character of these ales," said Stanners, who studied microbiology at the University of Guelph and learned brewing at the Siebel Institute of Brewing.

In a book specially printed for Molson's 150th anniversary, John Molson
is described as typically wearing a homespun suit and tuque, not
top hat and tails. Perhaps the writer took some license!

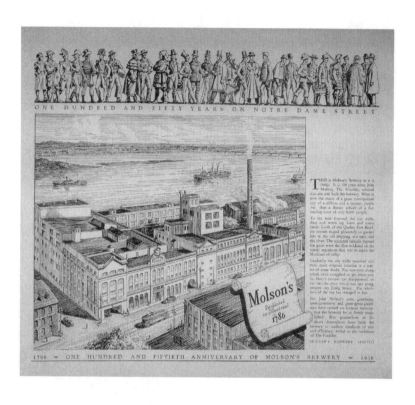

The Molson Brewery sat on the St. Lawrence River at St. Mary's Current. Molson was Canada's first steamship owner and his boats would pass his brewery on their way to Trois-Rivières and Quebec City.

Most of John Molson's sales were in mild ale, also called table beer or small beer. "These were made from a weaker mash and by steeping a strong mash a second or third time, and naturally they brought a lower price," writes Merrill Denison in *The Barley and the Stream*, a biography of the Molson Brewery. Small beer was the equivalent of what Quebecers in the late eighteenth century were brewing at home, made with malt and adjuncts like bran, molasses, sugar, honey and flavorings that included sassafras, ginger, and spruce.

John Molson would have made his own malt, before he found someone to do it for him at the right price. "And depending on how it was kilned, it could have been as dark as present-day Rickard's Red, or lighter. There was a whole range of colours," Stanners said.

Indeed, there was a range of colours even within one type or style of beer. Porters are probably the best case with which to illustrate this, Stanners showed. As brewing developed, different grades of beer were established. We see this in the common (or strong), small and table beers that John Molson himself brewed. "As the wort was made thinner and thinner, the first, second and third threads or grades separated. The heavy wort was the number one thread, diminishing to the third thread, that was made for porters"—those people who did the heavy lifting around the brewery. These workers couldn't afford the expensive, stronger-in-alcohol beer. "It became known as porter, but it was really just a grade of beer."

Porter was a favourite drink of the American Revolutionaries like George Washington and Thomas Jefferson, who made their own. But, Stanners was quick to point out, there's a world of range between what they and brewers made. "Every brewer that existed in every little town was making beer in a fashion after which he called porter," Stanners said. But colour, bitterness, and intensity varied greatly.

The trick back then, and which remains the trick now for brewers like Stanners, is consistency within the brewery. There's no point in making a good beer on Tuesday, a mediocre one on Wednesday and an exceptional one on Thursday, Stanners points out in a CD-ROM virtual tour of Molson Brewery. You have to make exceptional beers day in and day out.

Then, as now, Molson priced its beer to move. Molson ale, the standard beer of commerce, as that of other common brewers, was a strong beer of about six percent to eight percent alcohol. Strong beer sold for nine cents a bottle. A mild ale cost seven cents, and the table, or small, beer cost five cents per bottle.

John Molson must have sold quite a few of those nine- and five-cent bottles. The man described as Montreal's first modern industrialist "would often wear a homespun suit with a blue tuque [in his brewery], but in the evening, when going out, he would appear in a black suit with a white waistcoat and wear eye glasses with a long black ribbon attached," according to a privately published history, *John Molson's Brewery* (1936). He was a man of style, making his mark on his adopted city. Of course, the low wages the brewery paid—probably not out of line with the wages other industries at the time paid—kept him and his family suitably fashionable. In 1897, more than sixty years after the patriarch died, the brewery had seventy-five workers. The brewmaster was the best paid at two dollars a week. Most of the others made about $1.10. In the bottling department, the pay was sixty cents a week, but that's because the bottlers included women. The workweek was between sixty and sixty-two hours.

Little changed in brewing between John Molson's time and that of his grandson J.H.R. Molson, who ran the company until his death in 1897. J.H.R.'s brewmaster, John Hyde, would keep the spent grains outside the brewery for twenty-four hours, during which time local farmers were allowed to come by and take whatever they could haul away to use as feed for their cattle. It was a narrow window of opportunity; once the day was up, the grains would be removed before fermentation began and the accompanying signature smell annoyed neighbours.

Brewing took place seven or eight months out of the year. Can you imagine a summer without beer? But that's the way it was before refrigeration. Since the boiled, watered-down wort needs to cool down before yeast can be added, breweries didn't always operate in the summer months. One way to lower the temperature quickly was ice. Great blocks of ice, measuring about thirty-six cubic feet, were cut from the frozen St. Lawrence River during the winter, kept in an underground cellar at Molson Brewery, then used as long as they lasted in the summer when the temperature of city water rose above fifty degrees Fahrenheit.

Molson's first advertisement was published in 1803 in Montreal's *Gazette* newspaper. Early beer advertising emphasized the healthful aspects of drinking beer, as it did in later years when the brewers argued against Prohibition.

Nineteenth-century Brewers

Along the St. Lawrence River were other brewers, including several whose names we still recall, particularly Dawes' Black Horse Brewery and Dow & Company, both established within twenty years of Molson's—Dow in

Dawes Breweries, Export Ale, 1930s—the magnificent black Percheron
was synonymous with Black Horse Ale in Quebec.
Celebrating the 150th anniversary of Dow brewery in 1940.
For a while, neck labels on Boswell Ale claimed: "Canada's First Brewery, Founded
1668." After a competitor threatened to sue, the text was revised: "On the Site of
Canada's First Brewery." During the Second World War, when beer was rationed and
sent to the troops overseas, small shipments of Champlain Ale reached the thirsty
Montreal market, and eased the shortage.

Ekers Bohemian Lager label from the 1920s.
The Union Brewery was formed after the death of John Atkin, in 1896.
Montreal agent, B.Richer, offered several anti-smallpox products for sale,
including Labatt's India Pale Ale and xxx Stout.
Reinhardt's brewery was located at 529, City Hall Avenue (Hôtel-de-Ville). After
joining National Breweries in 1909, the small operation was shut down the following
year. The label claimed the brewery was established in 1852, but there
is no evidence of this in Montreal directories.

Laprairie and Dawes in Lachine. Both eventually moved to Montreal.

The nineteenth century was a fertile time in Quebec City brewing, a golden age really, nurtured by British immigrants who owned the breweries and drank the ale. The St. Roc Brewery, established as a distillery and then becoming a maker of spruce beer, was also known as the Quebec and Halifax Co. Brewery. Robert Lester founded the Cape Diamond Brewery in 1800 and sold it to Thomas Dunn who deeded it to Peter Bréhaut in 1816. By 1830, it belonged to John Racey, who also owned a brewery that bore his name.

These breweries were all in the Lower Town. They were joined by four more, including one founded in 1824 by Benjamin Tremain; another opened in 1821 by Thomas Wilson; a brewery started also in 1821 by Rémi Quirouet; and John Racey's operation, which opened in 1828. Within ten years all were gone but for Racey's, which was sold to Joseph Knight Boswell in 1843.

Across the way from St. Roc's, Duncan McCallum built a brewery in 1840. Established 65 years before, McCallum's was the leading brewery in Quebec City before being sold to Thomas Lloyd and Paul Lepper in 1845. This partnership also operated the St. Charles Brewery from 1842 to 1870. John Molson's heirs tried to establish a foothold in Quebec City in 1857 by purchasing the old McCallum site from Lloyd and Lepper, but they unloaded it in 1866 to William Drum. About the same time, Henry Joseph Jameson owned a brewery in the Ilot Saint-Nicholas section of the city.

Proteau and Carignan, which lasted a brief eleven years at the end of the nineteenth century, occupied the site of the former St. Roc Brewery. The Racey Brewery that Boswell bought in 1843 closed in 1952. Boswell, originally from Dublin, Ireland, had a great sense of history. Early on, he moved the brewery from St. Paul Street to the site of the old Palais de l'Intendant, which had once housed Jean Talon's Brasserie du Roi.

None of these breweries was large, and were much like today's microbreweries. From the 1800s through the 1950s, the McCallums, Lloyd and Leppers, and Raceys of the industry were the microbrewers. Fox Head Brewery, for example, owned by Amyot and Gauvin, produced but 58 quarts per day. Another, the Champlain Brewery, founded in 1911, produced 125 barrels of beer a day until it closed in 1952.

The Larger Breweries

Dow Brewery operated on the same site of the former Boswell Brewery in Quebec City, though its origins are in Montreal. William Dow, a Scot, became a partner of James Dunn, a miller from Laprairie, in establishing Dunn and Dow. Dunn came to the partnership with a brewing plant on Chaboillez Square on Notre Dame St. West. Records show that it had been purchased by John Stephenson in 1810 who then sold it to Dunn in 1818. Dunn and Dow began operations in November 1829. The Dow beer made in small quantities by Molson today can be traced to an 1867 recipe.

The Labatt name entered the Canadian brewing scene in London, Ontario, in 1847. It would be more than a hundred years before it set up a brewery close to Montreal, in the city of LaSalle. Now, it seems like Labatt's has always been part of the family. (It is part of my family, in fact. Uncle Gilbert Beauchemin worked for Labatt for a good thirty years. The whole family switched from Molson to Labatt when he started there.)

Other Montreal-area breweries were Thomas Dawes, founded in Lachine in 1825; the Ekers Brewery on St. Lawrence Street, 1845; the Montreal Brewing Co. established by the Cushing family before 1876; the Union Brewery between St. Dominique and Cadieux streets. below Sherbrooke Street; the Reinhardt Brewery on Hotel de Ville above Ontario Street; and the Imperial Brewery, whose buildings became the Dawes Brewery when Dawes moved to Montreal.

Within a decade of Canada's Confederation in 1867, beer was being brewed from sea to sea. In 1870, there were 143 brewery licenses in Canada, with production per plant averaging 50,000 gallons. (In 1870, the same amount of beer was produced by 3,286 licensed brewers in the United States. That year in the United Kingdom, there were 32,682 brewers.) Five years later, the number of brewers in Canada had jumped to 164. It has never been that high since.

As the number of breweries grew, so did the industry's importance to the Quebec economy. Beer's place at the table earned some respectability too. The minutes of a February 28, 1809, meeting at Montreal's exclusive men's-only Beaver Club, showed that the twenty-four members drank thirty-eight bottles of wine and twenty-six bottles of beer. At that time, brewing was Montreal's fourth largest industry with more than $27 million in capital, 1,820 employees and production valued at $14,724,116.

The Temperance Movement

The most serious threat to alcohol consumption in Quebec came in the mid-1800s. Its effects are still felt today tied as the French-Canadian temperance movement was to national pride and unity. Concern about people's drinking habits was in the air. One temperance society suggested that limiting men to six drinks a day was moderation. The bishop of Montreal, Ignace Bourget, believed in abstinence and recruited priests throughout the province to promote the message. The most effective of his acolytes was the curé Charles Chiniquy, who, between 1848 and 1851, through the power of his oratory persuaded 400,000 people, half of the population of Quebec, to give up booze. Such was this man's power that a town's tavern would close in anticipation of his visit to a parish and remain shuttered when he left. The Morris family brewery in Sainte Thérèse de Blainville, north of Montreal, was almost put out of business by Chiniquy after a one-week retreat in the parish church. The brewery's customers, overcome by Chiniquy's message, took the pledge of temperance, returned their kegs to the beermaker and claimed their deposits. In 1847, the year before Chiniquy's crusade began, distilleries in Quebec (then known as Canada East) made 645,386 gallons of liquor. In 1850, the figure was 79,914 gallons. Molson's, which in addition to its brewery, ran a distillery for many years, reported a loss in 1849 of £15,000.

Chiniquy was not subtle. His point was quite clear. The drink would cause French Canadians to lose their farms, their jobs and their livelihoods to the British, Scottish, Irish, and U.S. immigrants who already controlled the pursestrings in the larger cities, especially Montreal. Chiniquy's campaign ended abruptly in 1851, when Bourget discovered that although alcohol didn't tempt the young priest, women did. Bourget sent Chiniquy to Detroit. There, and in Chicago, he became involved in similar sex scandals. He was tried for perjury in Chicago and defended in court by Abraham Lincoln. Eventually he was excommunicated, became a Presbyterian minister, married, and returned to Quebec pulpits to blast the Catholic Church, even writing a book claiming Jesuit priests had conspired in the assassination of the U.S. president. He died in 1899 and is buried in Montreal's Côte-des-Neiges cemetery.

When Chiniquy left, the Catholic temperance movement lost its guiding light. Taverns opened and distilleries cranked up production, although Molson's distillery closed in 1866 at the height of its profitability because of high taxes. The Catholic Church, however, remained a social, moral, and political force in Quebec, including the next attempt at prohibition.

Over the next three decades, Canada lost perhaps forty breweries. This was partly because of pressure from prohibitionists in English Canada and the first stirrings of the women's movement in the form of the temperance society. In the 1840s women in English Canada were the principal fund-raisers and speakers for the temperance movement. Women sold the *Canadian*

When the temperance movement was strong, around 1920, P. Poulin
offered a non-alcoholic beverage, called "temperance beer."
Wanna Beer, from the World War I period.
Nurses at the Royal Vic would serve stout to patients (circa 1930).
J.M.S. Lager. Rare label from J.M. Spenard, from about 1912. The Spenard
brewery was located on St. Marguerite Street in Trois-Rivières.

Temperance Advocate door-to-door. The first national effort to ban the sale of alcohol throughout Canada came in the late 1800s. If it had not been for the Quebecer who was prime minister at the time, Sir Wilfrid Laurier, all of Canada would have entered the 1900s as a prohibitionist country. Canada voted on the isssue in 1898.

The Catholic Church in Quebec remained a voice of moderation. It stood aside as the banner-carrying liquor trade warned Quebec's overwhelmingly Catholic population that should prohibition become law, they might be denied the wine used at the Eucharist. Barring alcohol sales would also affect jobs, Quebecers were told. In 1897, brewers in the province spent $2,208,645 on grain, $360,000 on draughthorses, and $123,750 for hay to feed the horses.

When the votes were counted in September 1898, Quebecers voted eighty percent against prohibition. The other provinces favored it, winning by fewer than 14,000 votes. But Laurier dismissed the plebiscite results. Only forty-four percent of the registered voters had bothered to exercise their right, he said, and what kind of majority is that?

A Technological Breakthrough

The most lasting and important change to the brewing industry since the introduction of hops in the 1500s was refrigeration. Introduced in the early 1900s, it allowed brewers to brew year round without relying on ice, to more rapidly cool the boiled wort and introduce yeast to begin fermentation, and to market their products beyond their locale. Brewers could become regional for the first time.

The economic advantages of a regional brewery were not lost on Andrew Dawes, William's son. In 1909, he founded National Breweries Ltd., which saw Dawes, Dow, seven other breweries in Montreal, five breweries in Quebec City and Douglass & Co. in Terrebonne join forces in a stab at creating a monopoly. It didn't work. Molson, which had twenty percent of the Montreal market, refused to give up the family name.

Prohibition

The zealous prohibitionists wouldn't go away. A generation after the 1898 vote, prohibition knocked over the provinces like dominoes. First were Alberta, Manitoba, Ontario, and Nova Scotia in 1916; Saskatchewan, British Columbia, and New Brunswick followed in 1917. The federal government barred the use of grain for making beer in November of that year because it was needed to supply troops fighting in the First World War. In 1918, the federal cabinet decreed that no liquor could be made or imported until a year after peace was restored. That same year it seemed certain that Quebec would succumb to prohibition as well and that would have meant the end to National Breweries and Molson. Instead, a law was passed allowing for production of low-in-alcohol beer, 3.5 percent by volume.

What saved Quebec brewers from an all-out ban was partly the ludicrousness of the arguments against alcohol. Beer was decried as unsanitary and mischievous. The Montreal Anti-Alcoholic League's president even went so far as to suggest that the war was the result of the Germans' fondness for the hoppy beverage. "The brutality of the German nation" was proof of the evil effect of beer. The brewers, though, publicized the studies of Dr. Henry Davy, president of the British Medical Association, who is reported to have said: "Bread, cheese and beer for a meal is infinitely more scientific than the American meal of bread, tea and jam."

The brewers also cast the prohibition question in revolutionary images, alluding to the *patriotes* of 1837 and the 1849 burning of the Parliament building in Montreal, and even to the French and American revolutions. They stressed the idea that only a people can decide what is best for itself. "Why can't Quebec be left to decide its own affairs itself?" the brewers' advertisements asked. Montreal's *Gazette* weighed in with an editorial using the same question as its headline.

The ploy worked. Lomer Gouin, the premier of Quebec, ordered a referendum asking whether light beer, wine, and cider sales should be allowed in the province. The press and organized labour aligned themselves with the brewers against the prohibitionists, who were flush with their success in drying out the United States and the rest of Canada. The Eucharist argument was made once again, this time by a member of Gouin's cabinet. The vote came April 10, 1918. It was reported that at some Montreal polling stations, not a single vote was cast in favour of prohibition. Quebec voted 78 percent in favour of allowing the sale of beer, wine, and cider. Beer's alcoholic content was limited to 4.4 percent. It was dubbed "temperance beer."

"There are three hundred thirteen taverns where you (if a member of the male sex) can sit and drink a glass of beer. ... It is a beer garden—a beer saloon. And if this does not satisfy you there are eight hundred and one stores, where you can buy beer by the bottle, case or barrel," said Mrs. Sinclair Lewis, wife of the novelist and journalist, speaking about temperance in Quebec.

Montreal was home to a number of underworld characters with ties to the likes of Dutch Schultz and Al Capone, furnishing them and, in turn, the United States, with alcohol (even though Capone is reported to have said, "I don't even know what street Canada is on"). The exploits of the mob booze-runners are memorialized in the works of many writers, including Damon Runyon's "Lily of St. Pierre."

Prohibition was short-lived in Canada. By 1921, British Columbia called it quits, though it did regulate alcohol sales by establishing a government liquor board that served as a model for other provinces. Quebec established its liquor board the same year. In 1933 the United States repealed the Prohibition Act, and by 1936, fifteen U.S. states had their own liquor boards. The "noble experiment" of prohibitionists was over. Consumer demand and common sense prevailed.

Homebrewing

Beer production rose, as did alcohol levels, but not for long. The Great Depression hit brewers, and the Second World War spawned production restrictions. Many Canadians turned to brewing at home during the Great Depression—thus saving money and enjoying their vices at the same time. Jori Smith, the great Quebec painter who spent much of her life in picturesque Baie Saint Paul, recounted homebrewing in Charlevoix during the spring of 1936. Marius, a friend of the family,

> came to be equally fond of our home-made beer. I can no longer remember how we brewed it, but I do remember leaving one batch of it too long under the trap door, which unleashed a series of explosions one day when the three of us were quietly eating lunch. Just like pistol shots, they were—bang! bang! bang! We found the cellar awash in beer and strewn with bottles and shards of glass. Marius laughed till he cried. That was the last time we brewed our own beer, although we did once try making wine with rowan-berries. What a disappointment that was! It tasted like mouthwash. Needless to say, that was one recipe that didn't make it into Marius' little notebook.

Microbreweries

The intervening years saw the consolidation of the market into the hands of fewer and fewer brewers, and the production of blander beers. About the only excitement from the major brewers was their ad campaigns—often sexually charged and funny, and almost always avoiding mention of taste. Today, there are breweries in every province, and Canadians have come to view brewers as an integral part of the country's prosperity. The Big Two, Molson and Labatt, are integrally tied, too, to Canada's cultural image. They are linked to professional sports as either sponsor or owner, and support concerts, tours of recording artists, and music and arts festivals.

In the late 1970 in the United States, changes in legislation allowed for homebrewing and the licensing of local and regional brewers. Primary among these was the Boston Beer Co., makers of Samuel Adams, but the movement really took off in California, where Pete's Wicked Ales are made. From Massachusetts to California, artisanal beers found fans in the rest of the United States, then subsequently moved north to Vancouver before being adopted in Quebec. The rallying cry of all the microbreweries has been taste. Not for them the bikinis that sell Budweiser and Molson.

Several "generations" of microbrewers now exist in Quebec. The grand-daddy is the Golden Lion brewpub, which opened in 1986 as part of a restaurant in Lennoxville, in the Eastern Townships near Sherbrooke. A year later, Jérôme Denys obtained the first craft-brewing permit in Montreal for Le Cheval Blanc, a pub he had inherited on Ontario Street on the fringe of Montreal's Latin Quarter. For another year, the craft brewing scene was limited to these two pubs. The seed was sown, however, and it was not much longer before people searched for more locally made draught beers.

In 1987, three men in Quebec City, Pierre Turgeon, André Jean, and Roger Roy set up shop in an old warehouse in Quebec City's Lower Town, establishing L'Inox, now an "ecomusée," one of a group of museums that highlight traditional Quebec crafts like cheese-making, papermaking, framing, and now brewing.

Les Brasseurs GMT, founded in the Plateau section of Montreal by three former restaurateurs, answered the call for draught beers in the spring of 1988 with Belle Gueule, a lager. Following quickly on GMT's heels was Les Brasseurs du Nord, based in Blainville north of Montreal, whose Boréale Rousse, also available only on draught in those early days, really shook up the scene. First, it was an ale in a sea of lagers and bland ales. Second, it wasn't golden; it wasn't straw-coloured; it was copper. And third, it was brewed by Laura Urtnowski, a woman in a sea of male brewers.

Laura and Brasseurs du Nord were not alone for very long. McAuslan Brewing may be named after founder Peter McAuslan, but it was his wife,

Belle Gueule was introduced in 1988 by Les Brasseurs GMT.
Introduced in 1989, St. Ambroise Pale Ale was the first of the microbrewery
beers in Quebec to be bottled.
Blanche de Chambly is a bottle refermented wheat beer on lees, the first of
Unibroue's Belgian-inspired ales.
Unibroue's Maudite, with 8% alcohol content, can keep five years.

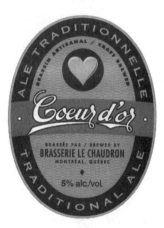

Boreale Rousse is a pure malt ale, the pride of Laura Urtnowski, president
and brewmaster of Les Brasseurs du Nord.
Jérôme Denys obtained the first craft-brewing permit in Montreal for Le
Cheval Blanc, a pub he had inherited on Ontario Street.
When Denys Tremblay declared himself King Denys I of L'Anse-Saint-Jean,
the brewery marked the occasion by producing Royale de l'Anse.
Coeur d'or, the flagship beer of Brasserie Le Chaudron, derives its name from
the pale-coloured malt used in its production.

Ellen Bounsall, who was the brewer. Her first beer, developed with British brewmaster Alan Pugsley, was St. Ambroise Pale Ale, whose distinct bitterness has become the signature taste profile of the brewery. Peter and Ellen like their hops. (It shouldn't pass without notice that the current brewmaster at Molson's Centre for Innovation is a woman as well—Nicole Derrick.)

McAuslan was the first brewery to bottle its product, the popular Pale Ale, which is named after Brother Ambroise, the Jesuit whose mandate was to make "cru and beer." This being Quebec, however, the street in the working-class Saint-Henri section of Montreal where the McAuslan Brewery is located is named *Saint* Ambroise and not *Brother* Ambroise. According to the city archives, the street was named in 1879 after Ambroise (340-397), the archbishop of Milan who instituted the cult of relics in the Catholic Church. But who's kidding whom? This is Montreal, Canada's beer capital. We know who the street was named for.

St. Ambroise Pale Ale came out in the summer of 1989. McAuslan also distinguished itself from GMT and Boréale beers by allowing a natural conditioning and not injecting its beers with carbon dioxide. GMT and Boréale, by injecting, are able to bypass a finishing stage in which carbon dioxide (CO_2) is naturally produced. Injection allows for a quick turnaround from the beginning of a mash to placement of a beer on a grocery-store shelf and does not adversely affect taste.

In the fall of 1989, in the working-class city of LaSalle, just down the street from the site of Labatt Brewing, a father-and-son team originally from Austria established Brasal Brewery. From the start, Marcel and Etan Jagermann were committed to brewing in the purest of beer traditions: Reinheitsgebot, the German Beer Purity Law of 1516, which means the beer uses no additives or preservatives of any kind. It is made with water, barley, hops, and yeast. From the start, Brasal offered its Hopps Brau German-style lager in bottles.

For the next three years the only change in the Quebec brewing scene was the decisions by GMT and Brasseurs du Nord to put their beers in bottles and on grocery-store shelves.

In those first years the commitment to bottling was the surest sign of confidence among the brewers after testing the floorboards with the draught offerings. As the beers grew in popularity, the brewers' share of the market grew, too, as did their need to get their products out to a larger area.

This is where André Dion enters the picture with a true change in the nature of the Quebec craft-brewing industry. The microbrewers asked Dion to help set up a province-wide distribution network. But Dion decided to set up his own brewery instead. With partner Serge Racine, he bought three-quarters of Massawippi, an existing brewery and brewpub on Lake Massawippi in North Hatley, and set up Unibroue as its distributor. A complete takeover in 1991 placed Massawippi under the control of Unibroue, which in the spring of 1992, hired Belgian brewer Gino Vantieghem and launched the first of its bottle-refermented ales, Blanche de Chambly. Like the others before it, Blanche de Chambly had initially been available only on draught. Robert Charlebois, an irreverent, working-class-hero type of Québécois rock star, bought into Unibroue about the same time.

Unibroue was from the start dedicated to Old World-style brewing. In fact the recipe and yeast strain used for its La Gaillarde (no longer in production) were said to date from the Middle Ages. Unibroue's high-in-alcohol ales are also distinguished by their longevity. Kept at cellar temperatures, the stronger ales of Europe can last up to twenty-five years. Unibroue's Maudite can keep five years; La Fin du Monde can keep ten years.

Unibroue also separated itself from the other Quebec microbrewers with the artwork used for its labels. With the exception of its Pilseners' bottle designs, Unibroue's labels stand up against the best of contemporary graphic art. So pleased was Charlebois with the artwork on the Maudite (a fiery, winged and horned devil), that the rocker had the artist substitute his face for the devil's and put it on all the publicity, CD and T-shirts included, for his 1993 tour, La Maudite Tournée. It got to the point, however, where it was unclear which was the marketing tie-in, the beer or the rock star.

Over the next four years came big changes, including a move of brewing facilities from Lennoxville to Chambly, exportation to Europe, the United States, and the rest of Canada, and an expansion of beer-making capacity to increase its annual beer production from 30,000 hectolitres to 180,000 hectolitres. By the end of 1996, more than 16 percent of Unibroue's beer was sold outside Quebec.

Brewing in the 1990s

The early 1990s were years of great expansion for Quebec's microbrewers. Between 1991 and 1994, the five first-generation Quebec microbrewers introduced twenty different beers representing fourteen different styles. Most put out new products every year. Brasseurs du Nord kept with its quartet—Boréale Rousse, Blonde (ale), Noire (stout) and Forte (strong ale)—as its stable of beers until 1999, when Forte was renamed Cuivrée and a honey beer, Dorée, was introduced. The brewery has pushed the all-natural image more than the other local breweries in its advertising, in its use of a pristine polar bear as its logo, and in the glacier-blue colouring of its packaging.

In 1993, Jérôme Denys' Le Cheval Blanc began bottling some of the fine beers he produced in his brewpub. He began with Tourmente and Titanic and sold about half the line through the stores of the Quebec Liquor Board.

In 1998, Unibroue began annual production of a special December beer, spicy and reminiscent of mulled Christmas wines, called the Don-de-Dieu and named after the triple-masted flagship Samuel de Champlain sailed, three hundred and ninety years before, to New France. Unibroue has intentionally linked its beers to Quebec's history and myths. One of its beers, 1837, celebrates the francophone and anglophone patriotes who rebelled against the British; another, Raftsman, honours the couriers du bois. In 2001 the company was allowed to indicate on its packaging that its products were free of genetically modified foods, a key issue in Europe.

Quebec's small brewers captured two percent of the beer market in La Belle Province in that short period. But that's a drop in the mash tun when one realizes that the two percent was split among six brewers and that Molson and Labatt breweries each corner forty-five to forty-seven percent of the market. The rest is made up of imported beers, particularly Heineken and Corona, brought into Canada by Molson. The figures are comparable to those in the United States, where artisanal brewers comprise three percent of the beer market, overwhelmed in sales but not taste by the biggies Anheuser-Busch and Miller.

With these figures, it's a wonder anyone would consider opening a microbrewery. But clearly, Quebecers thirst for difference. Also, the craft beer industry tends to be regional. The beers of Montreal haven't really caught on in other parts of Quebec, for example. Entrepreneurs saw a need in other areas of Quebec to produce quality, flavourful beers. Thus was the second generation of Quebec microbrewers born.

Beauce Broue, from the Beauce region south of Quebec City near the Maine border, launched La Beauceronne in 1995. It followed up that strong ale with a pale ale, La Chaudière, and a maple beer, Beauceronne à l'Erable. The brewery was reorganized in 1996 and now goes as Ferme Brasserie Schoune.

Brasseurs de l'Anse, in the northern Saguenay-Lac Saint Jean region, introduced Illégal light ale in the summer of 1995 and Illégal Dry and Folie Douce, a blueberry beer, in 1996. When Denys Tremblay declared himself King Denys I of L'Anse-Saint-Jean, the Saguenay region, the brewery honoured the occasion by producing Royale de l'Anse. (Denys abdicated in

January 2000, but left no successor. The beer remains in production.) The owners of de l'Anse shook up the industry in early 1999 by purchasing GMT and Le Cheval Blanc. In effect, Brasseurs R.J., the new company, created opportunity for the three breweries, each maintaining its unique brewing standards, to distribute in a larger area of Quebec. The purchase didn't cramp any styles. GMT put out a Belle Gueule Pilsner in the summer of 1999 and Cheval Blanc brought out Rescousse.

Seigneuriale Brewery began producing its Belgian-inspired hybrid beers from Boucherville, across the St. Lawrence River from Montreal. Its Seigneuriale beer, bottle-refermented like all its ales, was named one of the best beers of 1996 by Stephen Beaumont in *Wine Enthusiast* magazine. Its other beers are Seigneuriale Blonde, Réserve and Triple. In 1998, Sleeman's, the Ontario-based regional brewery, bought a ninety-five percent controlling interest in Seigneuriale, but maintained a hands-off attitude. The purchase was to allow Sleeman's to make in-roads into Quebec without paying protective tariffs.

From Saint Hyacinthe in the Montérégie region about an hour and a half east of Montreal along the St. Lawrence, Aux 4 Temps Brewery introduced Stouque, Krystal Weizen wheat ale in 1996, then a succession of three lagers—Gargouille Blonde and Rousse and La Chope. BrasseMonde in 1996 came out with L'Infidèle, a Belgian-style strong ale, and La Nuit Blanche, a coriander- and Curaçao-infused beer the next year, before the Outaouais-area brewer folded in late 1998. Aux 4 Temps also has gone under.

The people of the Lower Saint Lawrence and Gaspé regions of the province, the farthest east from Montreal, not to be left out, got their own microbrewery in 1996, with the Bas-St-Laurent Gaspésie Microbrewery. Its first beer, La Chic-Chocs, was introduced then, but because of its distance from major urban centres, the brewery failed to grow beyond its area and in 1999 it folded.

In the past few years eleven more breweries were introduced, with some surprising and flavourful beers, but with limited distribution: La Barberie, Belge Brasse, Chaudron, Charlevoix, du Lièvre, Nouvelle France, Omni, Saint-Arnould, Saint-Antoine-Abbé, Breughel and Broue Chope. In 1999, Etan Jagermann of Brasal sold his brewing equipment to SteamWhistle, an Ontario outfit. He was hoping to sell the recipes for his beers to a Quebec brewer. Broue Chope closed within a year of its birth, but was resurrected six months later as a contract brewer and maker of Chimère. Breughel has the distinction of owning a brewery in Senegal!

Competition from the smaller, second-generation brewers was negligible, though each has a devout following. What has kept the granddaddy brewers on their toes is always trying out new beers, bringing out new products, exposing their wares at festivals like the international beer festival, le Mondiale, held in June at Windsor Station in Montreal, and international competitions, where they consistently win awards.

To further expand its production capabilities, McAuslan Brewing took on Moosehead Brewery of New Brunswick as a minority partner. Moosehead's forty-five percent stake resulted in a new brewing facility for McAuslan and the introduction of the Moosehead family of ales and lagers to Quebec.

Most exciting is that brewpubs have proliferated throughout the province. They make beer in smaller quantities than breweries and can experiment and offer a greater variety of beers. So it was that Quebecers first tasted fruit beers in brewpubs before these types of beers were available in bottles from the larger microbrewers. Now, almost all the major microbrewers have a fruit beer: cherry beers from Unibroue and Cheval Blanc; blueberry from de l'Anse; apricot from McAuslan. Brasal during one of the festivals in Montreal tried out—and had drinkers vote on—apple, peach, and banana beers before settling on Hopps Brau au Pommes.

Although the number of breweries has risen, and though each is experiencing growth—Unibroue, now considered a regional brewery as opposed to a local microbrewery, is publicly traded—the percentage of market share has remained pretty much the same. Imports, like Heineken and Corona, have taken off, and sales of these two popular beers in supermarkets and corner stores nibble at the craft brewers. The Wall of Two—Molson and Labatt—has not crumbled, but they have taken a nick or two. The big brewers have caught on to the craft-brewery phenomenon. Both bought shares in Canadian craft brewers and Molson added a honey brown lager, an India Pale Ale, and a cream ale to its repertoire in the Ontario market. In the Quebec market it offers Maibock and it has done well with the innocuous Rickard's Red, formerly a British Columbia micro. Labatt introduced a cream ale to the Quebec market. Molson and Labatt have always brewed beers outside of their normal light-bodied golden ale and lager portfolios, like the Labatt Velvet Cream Stout, Labatt Porter, and Molson's Porter Champlain (with a black-and-white sketch of Samuel the Explorer emblazoned on the label.)

Today the brewery industry is healthy; eight breweries in Quebec generated employment for 58,090 people in 1997, more than one percent of the total active workforce, and almost one-third of the people employed in brewing directly or indirectly in Canada. They contributed more than $3 billion, almost two percent, to the province's gross domestic product.

Entering the twenty-first century, Quebec microbrewers were producing more than seventy-five different beers under their own labels, representing more than twenty unique styles and substyles of lagers and ales. The brewers were also under contract to make at least a further dozen beers for other companies; some were unique recipes, others were recipes of established foreign brewers like the McChouffe Belgian strong ale that Cheval Blanc brews. In North America there are only two other regions that can claim the same depth and variety of styles—the New England-New York region, with a combined population of about 30 million, and California, with a population of about 25 million—ten times the size of Quebec.

Illégal was introduced by Brasseurs de L'Anse in 1995.
Named after Mary Travers-Bolduc from the Gaspé, La Bolduc
pays homage to her memory.

Passion

"Une p'tite bière?" My grandfather pretended to offer me a bottle of beer. He held it by its long neck, pointed the green and gold label toward me, the "50" as red as a sunburn. I was twelve and this was the summer of 1975. The family was spending the day at the chalet on the Rivière Nicolet, not far from Drummondville, Quebec. My grandfather joked like this often, testing the limits of his grandchildren's desires to taste the forbidden; or maybe he was being the generous man he always was with us.

I surprised myself more than him. I grabbed the bottle. It was cool and damp like a cellar's stone wall. I tried to twist the bottle cap off as I'd seen it done by my grandfather, my father, my uncles countless times that day, and days before. I couldn't do it. My grandfather opened it and thrust it forward. He placed his hand atop my head, smiled and turned back to the adults, oblivious to the coming of age that had just transpired. I had a few sips, then set the bottle aside. I'd thought that even though the first sip was bad, I'd get used to it, but it took me a couple of years to like it, and it took me many more years after that to appreciate the look and sound, the smell and feel, the taste and aftertaste of a good beer.

My appreciation continues to grow—not just with more knowledge about brewing and beer styles, but by living—because living makes a life; it colours the work we do, the friends we make, the beers we choose. At many of the passages in my life, beer has been there, as much a presence as my friends. And though sometimes the temptation might have been there to drink myself into oblivion, it's better to rely on the friends.

On and off for five years beginning in 1985, my friend Ken Beaulieu and I were In Search of Neon. Our goal was simple: to visit and have one beer in each of the 351 municipalities of Massachusetts. The red, white and blues of the electric lights (it's been a long time since any bar actually had a true neon-gas light) guided us from Methuen to Monson, Stockbridge to Boston. One town, one beer. Our intentions were to discover the state, meet people and drink. They were good intentions for twenty-somethings and we drove many roads to fulfill them.

In fact, between March 1985 and August 1990, we drank in more than one-third of the state—124 towns—beginning at the Turners Falls Pizza House in Montague and ending at my friend Mary Helen's home in Marshfield, a going-away party as I was leaving for Montreal.

Those were the days before the proliferation of microbreweries and brewpubs. Our choice of beer was limited to the Bud and Miller family trees, including pale cousins like Rolling Rock, Genessee Cream, and Coors. When we felt like splurging, there was Heineken, Molson, or Labatt.

How much more interesting such a trip through the Bay State would be now. Across Massachusetts, there are more than twenty craft brewers. Restaurants in Richmond and bars in Braintree serve lagers and ales brewed locally or from across the state and New England. Beers like Samuel Adams cream stout, Berkshire porter, Catamount amber or Shipyard pale ale—beers whose meaning you feel in your mouth.

More than anything probably, In Search of Neon cemented our friendship and gave Ken and me memories of youthful excess to last a lifetime. On Sept. 29, 1985, according to the logbook I kept, we crashed a wedding at the Waconah Country Club in Dalton (no neon, but the other bar in town was closed). I still have Robert Hackmann's seating card. He was to be placed at Table 7. Ken convinced the best man that he'd gone to high school with the bride.

"Next round's on the house," we heard the bartender cry as we entered the Bonny Rigg in Becket later that day. What luck. But as we sucked back the long-neck Buds, it dawned on us that every redneck in the joint was holding a rifle. We'd walked into a turkey shoot, which is not a turkey hunt at all, but a reason to get drunk and shoot targets. The man with the best shot wins a Butterball.

I asked for a house gun.

"Ask them if the sights are good," Ken said. "They probably adjust the sights."

When the next round of shooting started, we followed everyone outside. I took my place in line and genuflected before the target, 20 yards away. I lifted the rifle, pressed the butt of it against my shoulder. I eyed the target in my sights. It moved. Or perhaps I did. I shot low and to the left.

"I really thought I'd done better," I told Ken later.

In 1988, we drank only once together, Bass IPAs in the Lenox pub on Boylston Street in Boston, where I was living. Our getting together was infrequent because the woman I loved didn't care much for the man I called friend. It must say something about beer and friendship that the thirteen towns we drank in the next year were after the relationship ended.

And it must say something about love that the woman I married gave me a beer-making kit as a wedding gift. The primary fermenter sat next to my side of the bed our first married year. The blub-blub-blub was a comforting background sound, my wife said, and she doesn't even drink.

On our wedding day, I served an Australian-style lager to my father-in-law, and in the intervening years have offered him my homemade stout, porter, a Samuel Adams taste-alike and an abbey ale, the recipes for which I also keep in a logbook. My father, perhaps less adventuresome, prefers the Pilsners, though I must admit I haven't made many of those. They just don't work for me any more.

One of the attractions of visiting my parents' home in Massachusetts, other than my parents, is the opportunity to drink beer I can't appreciate here in Quebec—whether it's a pale ale from Maine's D.L. Geary brewery bought in a package store or a pint of Noho pale ale served with lunch at Brewster's Court in Northampton. And what a surprise it was to discover that Holyoke, where I was born and went to high school and lived with Ken, was now the home of the Paper City Brewery, which offered an "Indian" Pale Ale, named after the Indian motocycle made in the area, and an Ireland Parish Irish ale, reflecting Holyoke's founding as the Irish parish of West Springfield in the late 1600s. One Thanksgiving, I bought my first beer from Upper Canada Brewery of Ontario in Chicopee, Massachusetts. It's not available in Quebec because of protective trade barriers. I put the bottles in a bag, packed the bag in my van and drove home to Montreal with it. At the border, the beers went undeclared—a proper, though small, nose-thumbing.

When Rafe, my father-in-law, visits from Los Angeles, he likes to drink Griffon Blonde, which he can't find back home. I hope still to introduce him to the plethora of Quebec brews now available: the dreamy and cloudy Unibroue products; the blueberry Folie Douce from Brasseurs de l'Anse; the regal Seigneuriale beers; and, of course, more of the hoppy McAuslan ales of which he is already fond.

The willingness to try any type of beer anywhere is part of the fun and part of the learning process. I belonged to a rather informal brewing club with co-workers. A few times a year, we gathered to sample each other's latest creations, whether it's ginger beer, mead, wine or ale. It was such a comfort to have these men at my dining table a number of years ago when, somewhere between the Danish Pilsner and the extra special bitter, I received a fax that my then-seventeen-year-old stepdaughter had just run away from her student-exchange program in Italy.

Eighteen months later, when my wife and I went to the former Soviet republic of Georgia to adopt a baby girl, I saw it as an opportunity to explore that country's culture—yeast culture included. I was warned by our hosts, however, not to have Georgian beer. It's of extremely poor quality, they said, which makes sense because in Georgia, one toasts one's enemies with beer!

Instead, we drank excellent homemade wine and brandy, Efes Pilsner imported from Turkey, and Russian vodka. On a return trip to Tbilisi in 1998, beer gardens proliferated in public gardens, serving draughts of Kavkaz (Caucasian) lager.

In England, on various visits over the years, I learned just how good an ale is when served at the proper temperature. The bouquet rises uninhibited, the mouth-feel is fuller, the aftertaste more crisp. My grandfather almost had it right: cellar temp is good for ales, like bitter, porter or stout. In his case, he was serving Labatt much too warm.

When my grandfather died in 1991, his life was celebrated by those of us remaining with a few "petite bières," Labatt's, mostly. And when my sister Monique was killed in April 1997, my friends were there to support me; inevitably, one would ask, "Get you a beer?"

Monique was living in Scotland at the time of her death. She was out with her boyfriend one Saturday, taking photographs of him as he rode on his motorcycle. Somehow, the motorcycle struck her; she was dead four hours later. I went to Scotland to claim her body, retrieve her effects, and take her home to Massachusetts.

Monique was nine years younger than I, and for most of our lives we hadn't had much opportunity to drink together. When I was of legal drinking age in Massachusetts, she was entering Grade Four. When Ken and I began In Search of Neon, she was a freshman in high school (and getting drunk at keg parties with all the other frosh). By the time Monique could drink legally, we were separated by 500 kilometres. She was in university, partying with her sorority sisters and the women on the crew team.

Before she left for Scotland in September 1996, Monique came to Montreal. The two of us went out for drinks at the Monkland Tavern. She matched me pint for pint, a pair of pale ales, a couple of stouts.

"Going to Scotland is a great opportunity for me to rethink what I want to do with my life," she said. All of twenty-four years old. Armed with a special visa allowing her to work and vacation for two years anywhere in Britain. Ready to taste life in a way that I envied. "Working in a pub would be fun," she said, and we drank to that. She paid.

Monique never got to work in a pub. She ended up doing what she'd done in Boston—analytical chemistry. But it turned out to be the right chemistry. She loved her job, she loved Scotland, she loved her friends. And she loved her Tennants, the way I grew to like it, too: tall, clear and cold.

Countless pints were drunk in Monique's name during those weeks after she died. With Ken and some childhood friends in Trumpets lounge in

Chicopee, the night before the burial, where Monique's best friend, Amy, showed off the pattern of her underwear. In Scotland, seven long days and nights before, where I drank with Amy, her Scottish husband, Mike, and his parents. We had Irish ale, a Sam Adams draught export unavailable in the States, a range of Tennants products, and Guinness. For dinner one night, I'd steamed mussels with Belgian ale, leeks, onions, and orange slices, a dish I'd just learned for one of our beer dinners back home in Montreal, and now wanted to share with these new, precious friends.

The day of the memorial, we drank to Monique at the Anchor Hotel in Johnshaven, Scotland, the words of the eulogist still fresh, pints all around, the Beatles playing on the jukebox. "Life goes on, bra. La, la, how the life goes on."

The Lees

Web Sites

The following Internet World Wide Web sites are excellent sources of information and fun.

www.brewers.ca
Brewers Association of Canada site includes product information, the On Tap newsletter, specialty beers, Canada-wide statistics, links.

www.bieranet.qc.ca
Bièr@net site is exclusively about Quebec brewers and their products.

www.boreale.qc.ca
Brasseurs du Nord site, product and business information.

www.unibroue.com
Unibroue's site include product and business information, recipes.

www.mcauslan.com
McAuslan's site includes product information, a virtual tour of the brewery, recipes and games.

www.brasseursrj.com
Tour info, products and history about GMT, Brasseurs de L'Anse and Le Cheval Blanc.

www.bieremag.com
Online version includes entire print issue of the magazine, with news, recipes, links and information on the Order of St. Arnold.

www.inox.qc.ca
Inox Pub (Quebec City) site includes info on the pub, plus a short history of brewing in the city and a virtual tour.

www.molson.com
Beer and sports. All Molson all the time.

www.labatt.com
Ditto.

www.canadawired.com/~sgignac/francais/menu.htm
Quebec Microbrewery Association site has information on beers, breweries, former breweries, virtual "collectibles," recipes and awards.

www.realbeer.com
The dean of Web sites on beer with news from around North America, links, games, a retail store and library.

www.realbeer.com/canada
The Canadian Beer Index is a chip of the shoulder of realbeer.com site but with 100% Canadian Content!

www.worldofbeer.com
Stephen Beaumont's site is chock-full of information, including personal favourites, recipes, news and feature articles.

www.beerhunter.com
The ubiquitous Michael Jackson's site.

www.allaboutbeer.com
From beer news and features to beer travels and homebrewing, even a brew pub finder, All About Beer, the online version of the successful magazine, has it all.

www.beercook.com
Lucy Saunders' website is as indispensible to foodies as her book *Cooking with Beer.*

Bibliography

I found the following texts helpful in varying degrees, in compiling the "History of Brewing in Quebec."

Baron, Stanley. *Brewed in America: A History of Beer and Ale in the United States* (New York: Little Brown, 1962).

Bowering, Ian. *In Search of the Perfect Brew in Ontario and Quebec* (Burnstown, Ontario: General Store Publishing House, 1993).

Brewers Association of Canada. *Brewing in Canada* (Ottawa: Brewers Association of Canada, 1965).

Campbell, Robert A. "Profit was just a circumstance: The Evolution of Government Liquor Control in British Columbia, 1920-1988," in *Drink in Canada: Historical Essays*, Cheryl Krasnick Warsh, ed. (Montreal: McGill-Queen's University Press, 1993).

Denison, Merrill. *The Barley and the Stream* (Toronto: McClelland and Stewart, 1955).

Donaldson, Gerald and Gerald Lampert, eds. *The Great Canadian Beer Book* (Toronto: McClelland & Stewart Ltd., 1975).

Douville, Raymond and Jacques Casanova. *Daily Life in Early Canada from Champlain to Montcalm* (London: George Allen and Unwin Ltd., 1968).

Eames, Alan D. *Secret Life of Beer: Legends, Lore and Little-Known Facts* (Pownal, Vermont: Storey Communications Inc., 1995).

Gibbon, John Murray. *Our Old Montreal* (Toronto: McClelland & Stewart Ltd., 1947).

Hamilton, Nick with Daniel Bilodeau. *Québec Beer Guide* (Montreal: Les Éditions de la Chenelière, 1997).

Molson's Brewery Ltd. *One Hundred and Fiftieth Anniversary of Molson's Brewery* (privately published by Molson's Brewery, 1936).

Molson Cos. Ltd. Annual Report, 1999.

Noel, Jan. "Dry Patriotism: The Chiniquy Crusade," in *Drink in Canada: Historical Essays*, Cheryl Krasnick Warsh, ed. (Montreal: McGill-Queen's University Press, 1993).

Roberts, Leslie. *Montreal: From Mission Colony to World City* (Toronto: Macmillan of Canada, 1969).

Siebel, Dr. John A. and Anton Schwarz. *History of the Brewing Industry and Brewing Science in America* (Chicago: G.L. Peterson, 1933).

Smith, Gregg. *Beer in America: The Early Years—1587-1840* (Boulder, Colorado: Siris Books, 1998).

Smith, Jori. *Charlevoix County, 1930* (Ottawa: Penumbra Press, 1998).

Snyder, Stephen. *The Beer Companion* (New York: Simon and Schuster, 1996).

Talon, Jean. *Memoir of Talon in Canada*, 1670, quoted in Zoltvany, Yves F., ed. *The French Tradition in America* (University of South Carolina, 1969).

Traill, Catherine Parr. *The Canadian Settler's Guide* New Canadian Library edition (Toronto: McClelland and Stewart Ltd., 1969).

Vaillancourt, Emile. *The History of the Brewing Industry in the Province of Quebec* (Montreal: G. Ducharme, 1940).

Woods, Shirley E. Jr. *The Molson Saga 1763-1983* (Toronto: Doubleday, 1983).

I used several books for information about beer, brewing, cooking with beer, or just for enjoyment.

Ayanoglu, Byron. *Montreal's Best Restaurants* (Montreal: Véhicule Press, 1999).

Beaumont, Stephen. *A Taste for Beer* (Toronto: Macmillan Canada, 1995).

———. *Stephen Beaumont's Brewpub Cookbook* (Toronto: Macmillan Canada, 1997).

Brenner, Leslie. *American Appetite: The Coming of Age of a Cuisine* (New York: Avon Books, 1999).

Brewers Association of Canada. *Cooking With Beer, Canada's Beverage* (Ottawa, Ont.: Brewers Association of Canada, 1998).

Buzzi, Aldo. *A Weakness for Almost Everything: Notes on Life, Gastronomy and Travel* (South Royalton, Vt.: Steerforth Press, 1999).

Colwin, Laurie. *More Home Cooking: A Writer Returns to the Kitchen* (New York: HarperPerennial, 1995).

Gould, Judith and Ruth Koretsky. *Brew Cuisine: Cooking With Beer* (Toronto: Summerhill Press Ltd., 1989).

Griffiths, W. Scott and Christopher Finch. *Famous Chefs and Other Characters Cook With Beer* (New York: Doubleday, 1996).

Harper, Timothy and Garrett Oliver. *The Good Beer Book: Brewing and Drinking Quality Ales and Lagers* (New York: Berkley Books, 1997).

Hesser, Amanda. *The Cook and the Gardener: A Year of Recipes and Writings from the French Countryside* (New York: W.W. Norton & Co., 1999).

Higgins, Patrick, Maura Kate Kilgore and Paul Hertlein. *The Homebrewer's Recipe Guide* (New York: Fireside Books, 1996).

Jackson, Michael. *Beer Companion: The World's Great Beer Styles, Gastronomy and Traditions* (London: DBP Publishers, 1993).

——. *The New World Guide to Beer* (Philadelphia: Running Press, 1988).

Katzen, Mollie. *Moosewood Cookbook* (Berkeley, Calif.: Ten Speed Press, 1977).

LaFrance, Peter. *Cooking & Eating With Beer: 50 Chefs, Brewmasters and Restaurateurs Talk about Beer and Food* (New York: John Wiley & Sons, 1997).

Lang, Jenifer Harvey, ed. *Larousse Gastronomique, American edition* (New York: Crown Publishers Inc., 1998 reprint).

McGee, Harold. *On Food and Cooking: The Science and Lore of the Kitchen* (New York: Fireside Books 1997).

Nachel, Marty with Steve Ettlinger. *Beer for Dummies* (Foster City, Calif.: IDG Books Worldwide, 1996).

Protz, Roger. *The Taste of Beer* (London: Weidenfeld & Nicolson, 1998).

Saunders, Lucy. *Cooking With Beer* (New York: Time Life Books, 1996).

Schermerhorn, Candy. *Great American Beer Cookbook* (Boulder, Colo.: Brewers Publications, 1993).

Snyder, Stephen. *The Beer Companion* (New York: Simon and Schuster, 1996).

Thompson, Jennifer Trainer. *The Great American Microbrewery Beer Book* (Berkeley, Calif.: Ten Speed Press, 1997).

Tolson, Berneita and Edith McCaig. *The Beer Cookbook: Beer—The Vital Ingredient in Hundreds of Exciting New Recipes* (New York: Hawthorn Publishers, 1968).

Recipes presented in *Salut!* came from a variety of sources. Most were provided by the microbreweries; several from Montreal chefs and friends; others from periodicals including *Les Bières Brassées au Québec,* which published once before folding. Chef Ronald Marcotte was the resource person on this Montreal magazine; *Sunset,* the discontinued cooking series out of California; and *Bon Appétit,* perhaps the most user-friendly of the monthly cooking magazines on the market.

Acknowledgements

I wish to thank the following people for their help on the recipes and for contributing to my understanding of beer and food:

Chef Christian Lévêque, Chef Eric Lehousse, Chef Rick Spensieri, Chef James MacGuire, Chef Ronald Marcotte, Chef Michael Lomonaco, Lucy Saunders, Stephen Beaumont, Dany Laferrière, Michael Shenker, Johanna Burkhard, Mario D'Eer, Marcy Goldman, Beatrice Cavaliere, Maria Cavaliere, Candy Schermerhorn, Gilles Jourdenais, Anne Gardiner, Ian Stanners, Peter McAuslan, Ellen Bounsall, Laura Urtnowski, André Dion, Jérôme Denys, Etan Jagermann, the Brewers Association of Canada, Helena Roig, and Denise Roig.

Also, Robert Mercure, Sharon Musgrove, Margo Pollock and John Alleyn. I wish to thank Frank Mrazik for the serendipitous e-mail that led to our meeting and an introduction to Canadian breweriana, some of which I am lucky enough to have included within the confines of these pages.

And lastly, the many people whom I have subjected to beer dinners and tastings: Sheila and Don, Gil and Linda, Mike and Monique, Mary Martha et Jean-Eudes, David, Bob and Mary, Ruth and Michael, Ann and Mark, Ariel, and Jacky and Rafe.

Index

A Taste for Beer 11, 112, 133
Abbey ale, definition of 17
Alaskan ESB 19
Alexander Keith's IPA 19
Algonquin County Lager 18
Allagash White 20; Triple Reserve 20
Amaretto Cookies 120
Amber and red ales, definition of 15
Amherst, General Jeffrey 148
Appetizers (starters) 28-39: Belgian Fries with Mayonnaise 33; Chinese Shrimp Rolls 37; Escabèche 32; Hummus bi-Tahini bi-Cheval Blanc 34; Kick-Ass Mussels 30; Mushrooms and Brie in Pastry 39; Mussels de Richelieu 28, Mussels au Gratin with Stout 29; Nessie's Riblets 36; Poppers and Fritters 35; Shrimp and Onion Rings in Belle Gueule Batter 31; Vegetable Plate with Boréale Blue Cheese Dip 38
Apple Blueberry Crisp 121
Apricot Chicken Pilaf with Almonds 70
Apricot wheat 17
Arkel Best Bitter Saranac Pale Ale 19
Artichoke Strudel 54
Atlantic Storm IPA 19
Aubergine and Pork with Belle Gueule Rousse 83
Aux 4 Temps Brewery 170
Ayanoglu, Byron 76

Baked Potato Soup 42
Balzer, John 92
Banana Bread, Blonde 109
Bass 19
Bas-St-Laurent Gaspésie Microbrewery 170
Baya Cavaliere's Spaghetti Sauce 65
Beauce Broue 169
Beauchemin, Gilbert 158
Beauchemin, Monique 174-75, 177-78
Beaulieu, Ken 174-77
Beaumont, Stephen 11, 21, 112, 133-34, 170
Belge Brasse 170

Belgian Fries with Mayonnaise 33
Bell's Porter 20
Belle Gueule 15, 18, 31, 73, 134, 164, 170; Rousse 15, 18, 65, 73, 83, 138-39
Belle Gueule Chicken 73
Beverages 138-40; Blonde on Blonde 138; Black and Tan 138; Black Velvet 138; Cherry Stout 138; Cocktail Bonne-femme 139; The Flip 139; Øl Grog 139; Panache à la Blanche 140; Prairie Oyster 139; Quelle Frappé 140; Red-Eye 139; Shandy 138; White Water 139
Bière de Noël 15, 19
Big Rock Traditional Ale 19
Big Rock Warthog Ale 19
Biscuits, Triple Wheat Beer 118
Black and Tan 138
Black Velvet 138
Blanche de Bruges 28, 81
Blanche de Chambly 16, 20, 28, 42, 51, 56, 60, 75, 81, 113, 120, 134, 138, 140, 168
Block, Adrian 144
Blonde Banana Bread 109
Blonde d'Achouffe 16, 133
Blonde on Blonde 138
Blueberry Pancakes 111
Blueberry Vinaigrette 55
Boréale Blonde 15, 19, 38, 80, 134, 138; Cuivrée 16, 20, 47, 88, 135, 168; Douce 17; Noire 16, 20, 29, 49, 97, 101-02, 123, 134, 168; Rousse 16, 64, 94, 134, 164, 168
Boston Beer Company 164
Boswell Brewery 157
Boswell, Joseph Knight 157
Bouceronne à l'Érable 112
Boucher, Pierre 148
Bounsall, Ellen 164
Bourget, Bishop Ignace 159
Braban, Pierre 147
Brasal Brewery 167
BrasseMonde 170
Brasserie de l'Habitation 146-47
Brasserie de Montréal 146-47

Brasserie du Roi 146, 157
Brasseurs de l'Anse 169-70
Brasseurs du Nord, Les 164, 168
Brasseurs GMT, Les 31, 164, 167, 169-70
Brasseurs R.J. 170
Breads: Blonde Banana Bread 109; Cranberry 108; Soda Bread 116; Trois Pistoles Rye Bread with English Malt Glaze 115
Bréhaut, Peter 157
Breughel 170
Brewers Association of Canada 37, 54, 59
Brewpub Cookbook 112
Brick Premium Lager 18
Brock's Extra Stout 20
Brown ale, definition of 16
Budweiser 164
Burkhard, Johanna 95

Calories 12
Canadian-style golden ale, definition of 15
Cape Diamond Brewery 157
Carbonnade à la Flamande 90
Carmelized Onion and Gorgonzola Pizza 113
Carrot and Sweet Potato Soup 45
Cartier, Jacques 144
Cauvet, Brother Ambroise 145
Cavaliere, Baya 65, 120
Cavaliere, Maria 65, 120
Celis Grand Cru 20; White 20
Chambly Chicken with Tarragon 75
Champlain Brewery 157
Champlain, Samuel de 144-45, 169
Charlebois, Robert 168
Charron Brothers 147
Chaudron 170
Cheddar and Ale Cheesecake 122
Cheese with beer 11, 133-35
Chemistry of beer 11-12
Cherry Stout 138
Cherry Zabaglione 129
Cheval Blanc 15, 169, 171; Legendary Red 16, 19, 52, 67; Original White 16, 20, 118, 138; Titanic 16, 20, 30, 106; Traditional Amber 15, 19, 128
Chicken and Tomato Salsa 56
Chicken in Beer with Endives 76
Chicken, Lewinsky 75
Chicken Sauté 74
Chilis: Lamb Chili 95; Mike's Chocolate

Chili 94; Red Line Chili 92
Chimère 170
Chinese Shrimp Rolls 37
Chiniquy, Charles 159
Chocolate Stout Mousse 125
Chomedy, Paul de 146
Christiansen, Hans 144
Climax ESB 18
Cocktail Bonnefemme 139
Colbert, Jean 145
Comfort Food Cookbook, The 95
Conners Best Bitter 19
Cooking with Beer 57
Corona 18
Coup de Grisou 16, 50, 61
Cranberry Bread 108
Creemore Springs 18
Crépeau, Pierre 147
Cushing family 158

D.L. Geary Brewery 176
D'Eer, Mario 29, 132-34
Damned Gazpacho 48
Davy, Dr. Henry 162
Dawes, Andrew 161
Dawes, Thomas 158
Dawes, William 161
Dawes' Black Horse Brewery 154, 158, 161
Denison, Merrill 153
Denys, Jérôme 169
Derrick, Nicole 167
Desserts 120-29; Amaretto Cookies 120; Apple Blueberry Crisp 121; Cheddar and Ale Cheesecake 122; Cherry Zabaglione 129; Chocolate Stout Mousse 125; Double the Chocolate Double the Fun Cake 123; Granité à la Folie Douce 127; Griffon Coffee Cake 126; Poached Pears in Traditional Amber Beer 128
Dion, André 167
Dogfish Head Midas Touch 20; Raison d'Etre 20
Don-de-Dieu 16, 19, 54
Dos Equis 18
Double the Chocolate Double the Fun Cake 123
Douglass & Co. 161
Dow & Company 154, 157-58, 161
Drum, William 157
Dunn, James 158

Dunn, Thomas 157
Duvel 20
Eau Bénite 17, 20, 32, 46, 62, 134
Eau Bénite Summer Cucumber Soup 46
1837 16, 20, 139
Ekers Brewery 158
Eldridge Pope Royal Oak 19
Ephemeral Salmon Pie 98
Ephémère 17, 98
Escabèche 32

Ferme Brasserie Schoune 112
Fettuccine and Shrimp with Chili Sauce 68
Fish and Seafood 28-29; 97-106;
    Ephemeral Salmon Pie 98; Grilled
    Antilles-Style Swordfish 106; Grilled
    Yellow Tuna Teriyaki 99; Kick Ass
    Mussels 30; Mussels au Gratin with
    Stout 29; Mussels de Richelieu 28;
    Oven-Poached Salmon with Herbs 97;
    Paella de Matane 84; Seafood
    Cassoulet 101; Scallops with Cous-
    cous 100; Stuffed Salmon with
    Stout 102; Trout Roulade with
    Asparagus 104
Fisher, Red 92
Flavoured or fruit ales, definition of 17
Flip, The 139
Folie Douce 17, 55, 111, 121, 127, 176
Fourquet Fourchette restaurant 132
Fox Head Brewery 157
French Onion Soup 47
French Toast 110
Fringante 16
Fromagerie Atwater 132
Fuller's Golden Pride 20

Gardiner, Anne 11-12
Gargouille Blonde 170; La Chope 170;
    Rousse 170
Gastown Amber Ale 19
Gazpacho, Illégal Black Bean 44
German Purity Law 167
Goldman, Marcy 116
Gouin, Lomer Premier 162
Granité à la Folie Douce 127
Granville Island IPA 19
Great Western Premium Lager 18
Griffon 15, 19; Blonde 37, 126, 134, 138,
    176; Brown 16, 19, 74, 86, 95, 104, 134
Griffon Coffee Cake 126

Grilled Antilles-Style Swordfish 106
Grilled Yellow Tuna Teriyaki 99
Grolsch Premium 18
Guinness 20, 29, 178

Halifax 1749 Stoned Fired Ale 19
Hariot, Thomas 143
Harpoon Winter Warmer 20
Hart Amber 19
Hart Festive Brown 19
Hébert, Louis 144
Heineken 18
History of brewing in Quebec 143-78
Homebrewing 163
Hopps Brau au Pommes 171
Hopps Brau lager 167
Hummus bi-Tahini bi-Cheval Blanc 34
Hyde, John 154

Illégal 15, 19, 36, 44, 138, 169
Illégal Black Bean Gazpacho 44
Inter-Continental Hotel 86-87, 127

Jackson, Michael 29
Jagermann, Etan 167, 170
Jagermann, Marcel 167
Jameson, Henry Joseph 157
Jean, André 164
John Labatt Classic 19
John Molson's Brewery 154
Jourdenais, Gilles 132-34
Juneau, René 104

Kalm, Peter 148
Kennedy, President John F. 122
Kick-Ass Mussels 30
Köld 18
Krystal Weizen wheat ale 170

L'Infidèle 170
L'Inox 164
La Barberie 170
La Beauceronne à l'Érable 20, 169
La Bolduc 15, 19, 35, 80
La Chaudière 169
La Chic-Chocs 170
La Chope 170
La Fin du Monde 17, 20, 68, 168
La Gaillarde 168
Labatt Blue 18; Porter, 171; Velvet
    Cream Stout 171

Labatt Brewing 158, 167, 171, 177
Laferrière, Dany 83
Lager, definition of 15
Lamb Chili 95
Laurier, Sir Wilfrid 161
Le Moyne, Charles 147
Le Petit Moulinsart 28, 81
Lehousse, Chef Eric 28
LeJeune, Paul 145
LeMercier, François 145-46
Lepper, Paul 157
Lester, Robert 157
Lévêque, Chef Christian 87, 101, 127-29
Lewinsky Chicken 78
Loyd, Thomas 157
Loch Ness 16, 20, 36, 92, 116
Lomonaco, Michael 102
Long Trail Hibernator Ale 20

MacGuire, Chef James 76
Maple Buttermilk Pancakes 112
Marcotte, Chef Ronald 106
Maudite 16, 20, 48, 100, 122, 133-35, 168
McAuslan Brewing 104, 164, 167, 171, 176
McAuslan, Peter 164
McAuslan's 39; Apricot wheat ale 45, 70;
  Scotch Ale 16, 20, 92, 116, 135;
  Vintage Ale 16, 20
McAuslan's Mixed Greens and Danish
  Blue Cheese Salad 59
McCallum 157
McChouffe 20, 133, 172
McEwan's 20
McNally's Extra Ale 20
McRogue Scotch 20
Menu planner 24-25
Microbreweries 163; beginnings (Quebec
  and U.S.) 164, 167
Mike's Chocolate Chili 94
Molson Export 19
Molson, J.H.R 154
Molson, John 9, 149-50; 153-54
Molson's Brewery 150, 153, 161, 169, 171
Molson's Centre for Innovation 167
Molson's Champlain Porter 171
Montreal Anti-Alcohol League 162
Montreal Brewing Company 158
Moosehead 19, 171
Moretti 18
Morris family 159
Mousse, Chocolate Stout 125

Mushrooms and Brie in Pastry 39
Muskoka Premium Dark 19
Mussels au Gratin with Stout 29
Mussels de Richelieu 28
Mussels, Kick Ass 30
Mystique apple cider 138

National Breweries Ltd. 161
Nessie's Riblets 36
New Belgium Trippel 20
Newcastle Brown 19, 95
Niagara Falls Maple Wheat 112
Nicholson's Café 78

Øl Grog 139
Origin of beer 9
Otter Creek Wolaver's Brown 19
Oven-Baked Berries Macerated in Blue-
  berry Beer 127
Oven-Poached Salmon with Herbs 97

Paella de Matane 84
Pairing beer 21-23
Pale ale, definition of 15
Panache à la Blanche 140
Pancakes: Blueberry 111; Maple
  Buttermilk 112
Paper City Brewery 176
Passe-Partout restaurant 76
Pasta 64-69; Baya Cavaliere's Spaghetti
  Sauce 65; Fettuccine and Shrimp with
  Chili Sauce 68; Penne with Spring
  Vegetables and Pecans 67; Spaghetti
  Sauce with Eggplant and Cinnamon
  66; Viva Italia Spaghetti Sauce 64
Penne with Spring Vegetables and Pecans
  67
Pete's Gold Coast 18
Pete's Wicked Pale Ale 19, 164
Pizza, Carmelized Onion and Gorgon-
  zola 113
Poached Pears in Traditional Amber Beer
  128
Poppers and Fritters 35
Pork Roll with Apples 86
Pork: Aubergine and Pork with Belle
  Gueule Rousse 83; Paella de Matane
  84; Pork Roll with Apples 86;
  Sauerkraut and Sausage with Royale de
  l'Anse 87
Potato Soup, Baked 42

Potatoes with Coriander and Blanche de Chambly 60
Potatoes with Rosemary and the Raftman 60
Poultry and Eggs 70-82; Apricot Chicken Pilaf with Almonds 70; Belle Gueule Chicken 73; Chambly Chicken with Tarragon 75; Chicken in Beer with Endives 76; Chicken Sauté 74; Lewinsky Chicken 78; Paella de Matane 84; St. Ambroise Chicken Curry 71; Turkey Tourtière 80; "U"nique Omelet for One 79; Waterzoie de Volaille à la Blanche 81
Prairie Oyster 139
Premium Lager 18
Prohibition 161-63
Pugsley, Alan 167
Pyramid Apricot Ale 20
Pyramid Pale Ale 19

Quebec and Halifax Co. Brewery 157
Quebec, History of brewing in 143-78
Quelle Frappé 140
Quelque Chose 17, 52, 57, 129, 138, 140
Quelque Chose Couscous and Napa Cabbage 57
Quirouet, Rémi 157

Racey Brewery 157
Racey, John 157
Rachbier, smoked 19
Racine, Serge 167-68
Raftman 16, 19, 60, 78, 134
Recollet fathers 144
Red Hook (ESB) 19
Red Line Chili 92
Red Potato and Fresh Bean Salad 61
Red-Eye 139
Reinhardt Brewery 158
Rescousse 16, 84, 170
Rickard's Red 19, 153
Roasted Squash, Carrot & Apple Soup 51
Rogue Shakespeare Stout 20
Roig, Denise 122, 125
Roig, Jackie 122
Roig, Raphael 10, 176
Rollet, Marie 144
Royale de L'Anse 15, 19, 87, 169
Rye Bread, Trois Pistoles 115

St. Ambroise beer mustard 58-59
St. Ambroise Chicken Curry 71
St. Ambroise Glazed Carrots 58
St. Ambroise Oatmeal Stout 16, 19, 29, 49, 76, 125, 138; Pale Ale 19, 39, 56, 59, 71, 99, 133, 167
Saint-Antoine-Abbé 170
Saint-Arnould beer 170
St. Augustine (of Hippo) 7
St. Arnold (Arnuf) 7
St. Bridget 7
St. Charles Brewery 157
Sainte-Paix (apple) 17, 20
Sainte-Paix (cherry wheat) 17, 20
St. Roc Brewery 157
Saint Sixtus 20
Saint Thomas à Becket 7
Salads and Sides 54-62; Artichoke Strudel 54; Blueberry Vinaigrette 55; Chicken and Tomato Salsa 56; McAuslan's Mixed Greens and Danish Blue Cheese Salad 59; Potatoes with Coriander and Blanche de Chambly 60; Potatoes with Rosemary and the Raftman 60; Red Potato and Fresh Bean Salad 61; St. Ambroise Glazed Carrots 58; Warm Salad of Smoked Duck 57, Smoked Salmon Salad 62; Quelque Chose Couscous and Napa Cabbage 57
Salmon See Fish and Seafood
Samuel Adams 9, 164; Boston Ale 19; Boston Lager 18; Cherry Wheat 20; Cranberry Lambic 20; Cranberry Wheat 108; Golden Pilsner 18; Scottish 20; Winter Lager 19
Samuel Smith Nut Brown 19; Celebrated Oatmeal 20
Saranac-Adirondack Amber Ale 19
Sauces: Trois Pistole Basting Sauce for Steak 89
Sauerkraut and Sausage with Royale de l'Anse 87
Saunders, Lucy 10, 57
Scallops with Couscous 100
Schermerhorn, Candy 125
Scotch ale, definition of 16
Scurvey 148
Seafood See Fish and Seafood
Seafood Cassoulet 101
Seigneuriale 170

Seigneuriale Brewery 170, 176
Serving beer 21-23
Shaftbury Rainforest Amber 19
Shandy 138
Shenker, Michael 94
Shrimp and Onion Rings 31
Shrimp Rolls, Chinese 37
Siebel Institute of Brewing 150
Sierra Nevada Pale Ale 19; Stout 20
Sleeman's 170
Sleeman's Orginal Dark 19
Smith, Jori 163
Smoked Salmon Salad 62
Snoreau 17, 20, 108
Society of Jesus 145
Soda Bread 116
Soups: Baked Potato 42; Carrot and Sweet
    Potato 45; Damned Gazpacho 48;
    Eau Bénite Summer Cucumber 46;
    French Onion 47; Illégal Black Bean
    Gazpacho 44; Roasted Squash, Carrot
    and Apple 51; Stout Minestrone 49;
    Strawberry-Cherry Cream 52; Yellow
    Pea Soup with Coup de Grisou 50
Spaghetti Sauce with Eggplant and Cin-
    namon 66
Spensieri, Chef Rick 39
Spruce beer 143, 147-49
Stanners, Ian 150, 153
SteamWhistle 170
Stella Artois 18
Stews and Chilis 90-95: Carbonnade à la
    Flamande 90; Lamb Chili 95; Mike's
    Chocolate Chili 94; Red Line Chili 92
Stouque 170
Stout Minestrone 49
Stout, definition of 16
Strawberry-Cherry Cream Soup 52
Strong ale 16
Strudel, Artichoke 54
Stuffed Salmon with Stout 102
Substitution chart 18
Sulpicians 147

Talon, Jean 145-47
Temperance movement 158-59, 161
Terrible 16
The Barley and Stream 153
The Inquisitive Cook 11
Theakston Old Peculiar 20
This is My Country Too 122

Titanic See Cheval Blanc
Tord-Vis 17, 20, 111-12
Tourmente 16, 20, 109
Tourtière, Turkey 80
Trappist ale 21
Tremain, Benjamin 157
Tremblay 12, 15
Tremblay, Denys 169
Tripel or triple, definition of 17
Triple Wheat Beer Biscuits 118
Trois Pistoles 16, 20, 89-90, 115, 135
Trois Pistoles Basting Sauce for Steak 89
Trois Pistoles Rye Bread with English
    Malt Glaze 115
Trout Roulade with Asparagus 104
Turgeon, Pierre 164
Turkey Tourtière 80

U 15, 18, 79, 134, 138
U2 15, 65
Unibroue 168-69, 171, 176
Unibroue's 11 16
Union Brewery 158
"U"nique Omelet for One 79
Upper Canada Brewery 176
Upper Canada Dark
Upper Canada Lager 18
Upper Canada Rebellion 18; Rebellion
    Lager 18
Urtnowski, Laura 164

Vantieghem, Gino 168
Veal Medallions with Boréale Cuivrée 88
Vegetable Plate with Boréale Blue
    Cheese Dip 38
Vinaigrette, Strawberry 55
Viva Italia Spaghetti Sauce 64

Warm Salad of Smoked Duck 57
Waterloo Dark Lager 19
Waterzoie de Volaille à la Blanche 81
Wheat beer, definition of 16
White Water 139
Williams, John A. 122
Wilson, Sue 11
Wilson, Thomas 157
Windows on the World 102
Wolfe, General James 148

Yellow Pea Soup with Coup de Grisou 50
Young's Oatmeal 20